826CHI *presents*

A SUNDAY AFTERNOON HOTDOG MEAL

A GUIDE TO CHICAGO FEATURING

shrimp from the future,

a park shaped like a spot of paint,

six-foot tall smelly, sweaty men,

a pizza crust that's humungous,

kind and friendly neighbors, and

cabs that smell like fresh flowers.

WRITTEN AND ILLUSTRATED BY 205 SECOND THROUGH SIXTH GRADE STUDENTS,
ALL OF WHOM ARE EAGER TO SHOW YOU AROUND. →

PUBLISHED JUNE 2007 BY 826CHI
COPYRIGHT © 2007 BY 826CHI
ALL RIGHTS RESERVED BY 826CHI
ISBN: 978-0-9790073-9-2
PRINTED IN CANADA
BOOK DESIGN BY MOLLIE EDGAR
ALL PROCEEDS FROM THE SALE OF THIS BOOK DIRECTLY BENEFIT
FREE STUDENT PROGRAMMING AT 826CHI.

WWW.826CHI.ORG

TABLE OF CONTENTS

3 **DINING IN**

4 **GETTING AROUND**

5 PARKS

7 SPORTS

ACKNOWLEDGEMENTS

OVER THE PAST six months, 826CHI staff and volunteers have visited forty-two classrooms around Chicago, and, in the process, we've collected over one thousand pieces of writing and artwork from students in the second through the sixth grades. When we began, we operated under the broadest of guidelines, asking students to write about what delighted them most, hoping that their collective vision would give shape to the book. When asked, for example, to write about something intriguing in their own neighborhoods, many students wrote essays that beautifully described parks, restaurants, and other special attractions. This broad request, however, also yielded one student's essay on her favorite teacher, Ms. Klink; it provided us with a feature on the outlandish, fanciful "Shrimp House," an eatery which just happens to be located in one student's own kitchen; and it presented us with our colorful, Chicago-style title, *A Sunday Afternoon Hotdog Meal*.

Each day when our volunteers met a new group of students, we entered their classrooms as lost tourists, desperately in need of a guidebook to Chicago. Heavily laden with bulky cameras and maps aplenty, our tutors claimed to be looking for destinations ranging from Baton Rouge to Peru. "Are we in Alaska?" one volunteer would ask. "No, I think this is Montenegro," another would reply. "But we're looking for Chicago!" a third, frustrated traveler would say. Our volunteers endured many sideways glances from students who couldn't believe how silly the group was behaving, but those students never failed to help us find our way.

Within this book, the work of 205 talented authors and artists is featured. Even in our most hopeful moments, we never imagined finding so many hilarious, informative, and poignant pieces. We know that many of these essays took shape because of the inspired vision and careful prodding of the following volunteers: Carrie Adams, Alissa Anderson, Adam Burke, Shawnee Barton, Lori Barrett, Mindy Bartholomae, Emily Bell, Elizabeth Boyne, Jennifer Brandel, Bailey Brittin, Jessica Bruah, Fritz Buerger, Christine Byun, Erin Carpenter, Rachel Claff, Carrie Colpitts, Kelly Connolly, Jason Crock, Erin Walter Curry, Jonathan D'Angelo, Erin Debenport, Shauna Dee, Jason Eiben, David Emanuel, Kristin Esch, Lisa Grayson, Cecilia Perez Hagist, Kirsten Hansen, Dan Hefner, Laura Heller, Kathryn Hines, Dan Hinkel, Linda Hogan, Sarah Holtkamp, Darrick Hooker, Allison Isaacson, Rachel Javellana, Jennifer Johannesen, Siggy Jonsson, Kyle Kartz, Juliana Keeping, Taylor Kelley, Chad Kenward, Meghan Keys, Jennie Kwon, Maria Lalli, Paul Lask, Rachel Lev, Hilary Lewis, Michele Lopatin, Stephanie Lu, Bridget McFadden, Galen Mason, Heidi Moore, Hayley Miller, Shannon Morley Milliken, Michael Munley, Chris Niemyjski, Laura Perelman, Daniel Petrella, Meghan Pierce, Claire Podulka, Kate Rockwell, Mike Schramm, Jessica Server, Rom Severino, Lisa Short, Emily Skaftun, Justin Skolnick, Sarah Smith, Sierra Sterling, Susan Twetten, Kate O'Rourke Udovicic, Lauren Wetherbee, Colleen Wilson, Kira Wisniewski, Michelle Yacht, and Laura Young. Most sincerely, we thank you.

This book also could not have materialized without the assistance of our Program Coordinator, Kait Steele, and our Outreach Coordinator, Patrick Shaffner, both of whom bravely took on additional work during the period that this project has been underway. We would have, furthermore, been lost without the careful guidance of Mollie Edgar who created the book's clever design and devoted so many hours to its production. And, it is not overstating our case to say that this book never would have existed without the infectious spirit and generous support of Matt Schrecengost. Lastly, extreme gratitude is due to Mara O'Brien, 826CHI's Director of Education, in almost unspeakable abundance. For guidebooks, there is no greater guide.

Because of the incredible enthusiasm that has been brought to this project by teachers, students, parents, volunteers, and staff, the production of this book has been almost mystically seamless. Granted, we've had a few odd moments that might not be usual occurrences at more staid publishing houses. It is probably not, for example, common to fact-check a restaurant's address by calling the front desk and asking, "Could you tell me if you have 'a fountain full of fishes', a 'diamond chandelier', and 'a rare display ship with a Japanese flag' on your cash register?" But, of course, we wouldn't want it any other way. We hope this collection of essays offers you both insight on how these students experience their city and the chance to see Chicago again, yourself, in a whole new light.

—*Leah Guenther*
EXECUTIVE DIRECTOR, 826CHI

OUR CONTRIBUTORS

We would like to issue countless thanks to the following schools and teachers for participating in this project and allowing us to meet their clever students. We would have remained lost tourists without your help!

BARTOLOME DE LAS CASAS CHARTER SCHOOL
1641 West 16th Street
Marisa Heilman

CHARLES S. BROWNELL SCHOOL
6741 South Michigan Avenue
Leslie Elfers, Laurence Jones, Megan Kelly, Diane Kemble, Darcy Maxim, Andrea Parker, and Megan Shea

CHICAGO INTERNATIONAL CHARTER SCHOOL | WEST BELDEN CAMPUS
2245 North McVicker Avenue
Jennifer Bartgen, Jennie Jacobson, Colleen Joyce, Selena Lynn, Amy Micari, Christina Monson, Jane Szot, and Victoria Tuzzolino

HANS CHRISTIAN ANDERSEN SCHOOL
1148 North Honore Street
Dee Collier, Joanne Hernandez, Carol Novak, Mary Jane Maloney, Persida Rivera, Elizabeth Ryan, Lezlie Schiff, Teresa Silva, and Cara Ziegler

LOUISA MAY ALCOTT ELEMENTARY SCHOOL
2625 North Orchard Street
Joan Billingham, Barbara Cameron, Jessica Klink, Megan Tomczyk, and Jenny Vincent

MARY E. COURTENAY LANGUAGE ARTS CENTER
1726 West Berteau Avenue
Elly Gonsalves, Pat Kiley, and Judy Metzger

NAMASTE CHARTER SCHOOL
3540 South Hermitage Avenue
Miriam Alvarado, Anabel Avitia, Brianna English, Andrea Frost, Jake Kelly, Heather LaMont, Lola Reese, Diane Scharnweber, and Allison Slade

RODOLFO LOZANO BILINGUAL SCHOOL
1424 North Cleaver Street
Concepción Calderon, Ann Cline, Bella Rudnick, and Colleen Scampini

1 | *attractions*

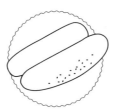

A BIG ROUND HOUSE
with a TELESCOPE

THE ADLER PLANETARIUM is close to the city and is on a little island. You take a trail to get there. The building is like a big round house with a telescope sticking out. The Planetarium is an interesting place to go because it is dark and can give you a creepy feeling. When I was in third grade, I went on an extraordinary field trip there.

My favorite part of the Planetarium is when you go into a room that is as big as a movie theater and as dark. You sit on spongy seats that move back, and when you look up you see cool constellations and planets. Then the staff takes you to a room where you can go to the meteoroid section, spaceship section, or spaceman section. All of the sections are exciting. In the planet section we learned that some planets are gas planets and some are rock planets. Then we went on a space walk where we saw the inside of a spaceship. We also saw meteoroids flying around and saw how meteoroids are made. The staff took out real pieces of real meteoroids to show us. When our field trip was almost over, they gave us souvenirs of spaceships and spacemen.   —*Isai Olivares, grade 5*

19

ATTRACTIONS

TAKE *a* TOUR *of the* SKY

ADLER PLANETARIUM IS located just down Lake Shore Drive, right on the lake. It has fun, educational movies about the sky, stars, and space. There are models of space explorers like Neil Armstrong and they also have preserved space ships. One of the movies they show is a sky tour where it projects pictures of the sky over periods of time. It shows what it looks like during different seasons of the year. It's my favorite. I learned that if you look at the Big Dipper or Little Dipper, and you pretend there is a hole in the dipper and a line going straight down from it, you can find the North (or South, or East, or West) Star. Also, did you know that sometimes you see a "splotch" in the sky and it's really another galaxy? You can actually see it with the naked eye!

Adler Planetarium really is a great place and you should go there on your next trip to Chicago. But be careful! Don't let the aliens get you!   —*Henry Post, grade 4*

In the third grade we went on a field trip to the Adler Planetarium. It was so much fun that when we were about to leave, we all said, "Awwww!"

—Jocelyn Villa, grade 5

SMELLS FRESH *and* FLOWERY

MY FAVORITE PLACE to go to in Chicago is Buckingham Fountain! It's really best to go in the summer. I like to go with my friends or my sister and we can get there by train, bus, or trolley. Some things I think you should bring with you to Buckingham Fountain are a camera, drink, food, film, and a laptop so you can do research.

The water at Buckingham Fountain can turn different colors and sometimes the wind blows the water. The air there smells fresh and flowery. There are rocks that are hard and pointy on the ground in front of the fountain. It's kind of like when you go to the beach and there are little seashells by the water that you step on. When you walk, you can feel the rocks and sometimes they get in your socks. There is also a garden that you can walk through.

Around Buckingham Fountain there are lots of different people. There are usually a lot of people who have never seen it before, who are just visiting. There are also a lot of rich people there, because they live close by in the downtown.   —*Diana Salgado, grade 4*

EVEN HAS *a* ROOM *for* DRAMA

THE CHICAGO CULTURAL CENTER is the most fantastic place to go. It is downtown by Millennium Park. I have been to the art room there. It is so fun. In the art room there are tables, plastic on the floor to keep the paint off, art materials, a piano, and a back door to get to another place. I went to the art room with my old class once a month. We made many different sculptures and pictures, and little people out of brown clay. It was really hard to make the clay into a ball for the people's heads, so we had to add water to it.

At the Cultural Center, there was also an art gallery there with pictures and mannequins. The mannequins had weird clothes on and weird hats. I liked them, but they were scary. Some pictures were illustrated by Pablo Picasso. One of his paintings was blue. It showed a graveyard with dirt, gravestones, a tree, and people that looked like zombies. It was scary and sad. The Cultural Center even has a room for drama. I didn't go there, but I walked past a room that said "DRAMA" on it. The people inside were moving around with their mouths closed, like mimes.

The Chicago Cultural Center is a fun and interesting place to go. Last year, I went there in September. I had to bring my own lunch because they didn't have a cafeteria, but it is still a good place to visit. I would say if you go to the Cultural Center you should bring food, a camera, and a backpack in case of emergency.

—*Sylvia Frank, grade 4*

TAKING GOOD CARE *of the* CITY

IN CITY HALL, Mayor Daley is sometimes there. He takes good care of the city and has good ideas. For example, Mayor Daley thought about the idea that Millennium Park should be built, then the construction workers built the park. One time, my family was going to City Hall to talk about immigration, but he wasn't there so we talked to the other people who work in City Hall. We wanted my father to stay with the family and we did not want him to have to go to Mexico and leave us alone. While we were talking to the people who worked there about immigration, they were taking notes about it and they said they would tell Mayor Daley.

If you are going to City Hall, you should dress up nice. If you go to City Hall during the holidays, you'll see they fix it up with ornaments. On the roof of City Hall, you will see a beautiful garden and fresh green grass. It is better to go to City Hall in a train because if you go in a bus or a taxi there could be a lot of traffic. You also need an ID to go to City Hall because there are a lot of security guards. Be prepared!   —*Jorge Santos, grade 5*

SEE CHICKENS EATING RICE

THE PLACE I LIKE to go most is the Lincoln Park Zoo. I have been there two times before and it was especially fun to look at the monkeys there. I would recommend going in the summer when it is hot instead of in the winter when it is freezing cold. There is a river that runs through the zoo and there are also trees and flowers. Some of the trees have names. When you go to the zoo, take the bus because for cars the parking lot will be full. You don't have to pay to get into the zoo because it is free. I think that's nice.

The animals I like most are monkeys, birds, and snakes. I also like the little farm that has horses, pigs, sheep, and chickens. Some of the animals will be resting where there is no sun, and some will be eating leaves. The last time I went to the Lincoln Park Zoo, I saw the monkeys hanging and swinging and they were having fun! One bird I saw was yellow. Some were black. And some were toucans with long beaks and red stripes. The snakes had rattles at the end of their tails and one cage of snakes had about five eggs in it. The horses were running around and you could see chickens eating rice. The zoo is really fun and the best part is when you get to go with your family. —*Jonatan Villa, grade 4*

One of my special memories of Lincoln Park Zoo is Monkey Day. It's when the zoo puts every single monkey in one place!

—Justice Smith, grade 4

BEWARE *of the* MONKEYS

LINCOLN PARK ZOO is phenomenal! The animals and the events there are out-of-this-world! The Lincoln Park Zoo has tons of animals such as monkeys, giraffes, hippos, ostriches, flamingos, meerkats, snakes, zebras, horses, and so many more! The best time to go is probably spring because you'll be walking a lot and the weather in spring is great for walking. Spring is also a great time for blooming flowers.

When I was seven, my mom and I were at Lincoln Park Zoo. I wanted to see the monkeys because they are my favorite animals. I like watching them because they're so human-like. To see them, we had to go to the monkey house. It is a place that has lots of trees, bushes, rocks, and a rope for the monkeys to swing on. We were watching the monkeys, having a good time, when the monkey on the highest branch...PEED ON ME! I couldn't believe it! So, what I'm telling you is that even though Lincoln Park Zoo is fun, BEWARE OF THE MONKEYS!

—*Kira Gallancy, grade 4*

illustration by *Gabriela Agguire, grade 6*

A MINI AMUSEMENT PARK

IF YOU ARE looking for entertainment, go to Millennium Park. Before you go, pack a swimsuit (later you'll find out why), a picnic, sunscreen, and money. My family always drives to Millennium Park, but if you want views, take the bus there. If you didn't pack a picnic, don't worry: you can buy nachos, hot dogs, and other food. It's delicious, too!

My favorite place to go is "The Bean." It is a bunch of mirrors shaped into a kidney bean. My brother and I always laugh looking at twenty of ourselves. The second best place is what I call the "Face Fall." It is about sixty cameras that show the face of a person. It is a waterfall to play in, too. If you want to get wet, go there. I always hear the sound of shrieking kids, the water crashing, cars, birds, and just so many other sounds!

When we first heard about Millennium Park, I wasn't too excited about going because I thought it was just going to be a bunch of statues and grass. But it turned out to be like a mini amusement park. We went with our grandma, grandpa, cousin, mom, and dad. We played tag and had a fantastic time because there were few obstacles. When it was time to come home we were all tuckered out from running around and looking in the mirrors.

Millennium Park also has free concerts. We went to a concert with Buddhist monks. They had really big tubes that made huge sounds, like brass instruments. —*Levi Todd, grade 5*

A THOUSAND DIFFERENT FACES

IF YOU SEE nothing else, the bridge and the Crown Fountain are the things you must see at Millennium Park. There's a snake bridge that you walk on for a long time and then you go into another park. The gardens have a pool that you can wet your feet in. Once there were dancers with lanterns and we saw a mallard (boy duck) in the big pool. The park also has a bigger pool and a lot of plants that you can look at. And next is The Bean, which is a big glass mirror that is shaped like…what do you think? A bean! We saw them polishing it once because there were lots of handprints on it.

The Crown Fountain at Millennium Park is two big rectangles across from each other that have on them a thousand different faces. In the summer time, we bring our swimsuits since the fountain has water shooting out. I must warn you, though, the water comes down very hard, hard, hard. Right before the faces change to another face, they close their eyes and spit out water. It gets crowded, so I'm not usually by the fountain when that happens.

In the winter there are other things to do in the park, like ice skating. You can look down on the ice skating rink from The Bean. Once, I ate at the restaurant in the park. I don't remember what I ate, but I give it a thumbs up.   —*Nicole Culver, grade 2*

GREAT PLACE *for a* SCIENCE FAN

HELLO, VISITORS, AND GREETINGS from the Museum of Science and Industry! The Museum of Science and Industry is a great place to be if you are a science fan, but even if you are not a science fan, you will fall in love with the attractions here. My favorite is a great flight simulator: it is a 727 jet. It simulates take-offs and landings. It is on the second floor. You climb into the passenger area of the jet. The cockpit is closed off. The guy pretending to be the pilot says, "Ladies and Gentlemen, please take your seats. This flight will take approximately three hours. Please buckle your seatbelts and secure your tray tables." You then buckle your seatbelts, but there really aren't any tray tables. You start hearing loud noises that are supposed to be coming from the engine and can hear the wind as the plane takes off. After ten minutes, the pilot announces things about the air, like the temperature and altitude. Then he starts landing. You hear the wheels on the ground and the pilot says, "Ladies and gentlemen, please don't unbuckle your seatbelts until we are firmly parked." Then you exit the plane. The whole thing takes about twenty minutes.

But there is more! You can also create a toy top with the help of robots in a factory! You feel like you are really in an assembly line! There is also a V505 submarine that you can look at. But the biggest attraction is the Omnimax Theater. Films must be purchased separately, but it is worth it because it is Chicago's only five-story, domed wrap-around movie screen. I've been there. I saw *Sharks: The Movie*. It was boring, but don't worry because it got discontinued. I just have to tell you one more thing—don't forget your camera!   —*Alejandro Ballesteros, grade 4*

A DAY *at the* FROG MUSEUM

MY DAD IS a cab driver and he drives his white cab almost every day. Sometimes I get to sit with my dad in front when there is nobody else in the cab. Once I was with my dad in his cab. I knew I was going to have a great day. My dad is great. He was going to take me to the frog museum, or what other people call the Museum of Science and Industry. I went to the frog museum one time before on a field trip and my dad was a chaperone then.

I waited until we got there and soon we did. I saw a frog movie about poisonous frogs and my dad bought me a frog book. But then I got lost. I was looking at some blue poisonous frogs and when I turned around my dad was gone. I couldn't find him. A security guard found me and took care of me for a long time. I felt nervous while I was waiting because I didn't know if I was going to find my dad. Finally, I saw him, though. Then I saw my mom. I was very surprised to see my mom because she didn't go to the museum with us but my dad called her when I got lost.

I ran and gave them both a hug. When we walked out of the museum I felt something small on my back and heard a croak. I thought I was going to leave with a frog from the museum following behind me, but it was my dad playing a joke on me with a small rubber frog.   —*Samantha Oviedo, grade 3*

illustration by Jennifer Garcia, grade 5

THE BIGGEST PLACE *in* CHICAGO

NAVY PIER IS the biggest place I know in Chicago and you can do whatever you want to there. There are many rides, and the tallest is the Ferris wheel. I would have to say that the Ferris wheel is a little bit slow, but it goes high up so that you can see all of Lake Michigan. It makes it look just like an ocean. Navy Pier also has roller coasters, which I like because they are fast and scary. One goes upside down and one goes underground. One time I went into the haunted house they have there but I didn't get scared. It wasn't horrifying. It was dark but it was only full of fake monsters.

When I got home from Navy Pier one night I had a dream about it. Being on the Ferris wheel felt like I was flying so, in my dream, I had special powers and could fly all around. In my dream, all of the rides were bigger and faster and I was allowed to eat all the junk food I could find without paying for it. It was incredible.
—*Eileen Salas, grade 4*

MANY DIFFERENT KINDS
of PEOPLE

NAVY PIER ATTRACTS travelers from all over. It is surrounded by Lake Michigan and has the Children's Museum and the Museum of Stained Glass Windows. There are also great smells from the refreshment stands that sell hot dogs and drinks. When you're there you hear many different kinds of people talking about where to go next.

Navy Pier has a giant Ferris wheel. At night, it is all lit up. Someday I hope to do it when the line is not so big. There is also a speedboat called the Sea Dog. It goes so fast! Water splashes everywhere! When I go to Navy Pier, I usually take Lake Shore Drive. My family and I usually go two or three times each summer and we bring snacks and water with us for when it is hot out.

One time, my friends came all the way from Minnesota to visit. We went to the Children's Museum in Navy Pier. We played in the water room and the digging-for-fossils room and everywhere else in the museum. After that, we got Dippin' Dots. When we ate all of those, we went to the Sea Dog speedboat and it was so much fun. Navy Pier is a great place to go in Chicago!

—*Katie Mendez, grade 5*

COOL *and* SLIMY
CREEPY CRAWLERS

THE NATURE MUSEUM is called the Nature Museum because there are
many cool and slimy creepy crawlers, and lots of animals too. The
Nature Museum is very popular. My class at school has a field trip
there every year and my parents take me, too.

Once I went to the Nature Museum's butterfly room. To my
surprise, butterflies were everywhere. I was kind of scared but
went through it even though it kind of worried me. It turned
out I liked it a lot. It was a beautiful sight. In the butterfly room
there are a lot of plants so that the butterflies can sip nectar from
their flowers. Some plants hang from the ceiling and others sit in
specific places.

The Nature Museum also has many different snakes but the
only snake I can ever pet is the corn snake. Its colors are red with
yellow stripes. It felt smooth and lumpy.   *—Faith Stein, grade 2*

LOOKS LIKE *a* GIANT MIRROR

WHEN I FIRST WENT to the Sears Tower it was foggy and the day smelled like a Sunday afternoon hotdog meal. I took the CTA train and then the bus to go downtown. At the top of the Sears Tower there is fresh air, and getting into the building is free. The Sears Tower is very tall and looks like a giant mirror.

If you want to know what to bring to the Sears Tower, I say bring a gas mask because there are a lot of people wearing smelly perfume and then you won't have to smell it. I would also bring a penny so you can drop it into Lake Michigan to see how big of a splash you could make. You could also bring binoculars to see all of the other buildings around you.

I thought about bringing a parachute with me once. I thought I could jump off of the building and fly but I'm afraid of heights so I don't think I'll do that.   —*Eduardo Vega, grade 4*

BOTH SCARY *and* AMAZING

THE SEARS TOWER is the biggest building in Chicago. It's one of the tallest buildings in the United States. On the top there are two antennas. On holidays, they're different colors and the red lights on top tell airplane pilots not to crash into the building.

The Sears Tower seems so big that you can probably fit one thousand people there. A lot of offices, computers, and people are there daily. I think it would be both scary and amazing to work on one of the high floors. Some people work there all day. The rest will go home after their visit or stay and eat at the restaurant in the lobby. The lobby has a gift shop too, and in this gift shop they sell key chains, shirts, and mini Sears Towers.

One time, my dad and I went there in the summer when I was five. It was awesome and fun! I saw my cousin KJ who works in the Sears Tower. He was in the lobby. He told us what is on all the floors. Some of them have offices and some of them have cafeterias. KJ then brought me to the top. The elevator went fast! I saw the John Hancock building, the AMC theatre, and the Dan Ryan. I saw a whole lot of people walking around on the ground. In the lookout area they have pictures of the Chicago fire and other interesting things. What was really neat was seeing the blueprint of the Sears Tower before it was built! —*Royal Washington, grade 4*

illustration by Hector Montalvo, grade 5

A LOT *of* WHISTLE BLOWING

THE SHEDD AQUARIUM has shows, sharks, and starfish. It's located near Lake Michigan. In third grade, we went on a field trip to the Shedd. It was crowded with students and all kinds of people.

At the Shedd, you can touch the starfish under water. Some look spiky; some look soft; and some are rough or hard like a rock. Some have an ability to change color to catch their prey. Some other fish confuse their enemies by releasing some glowing glue that traps prey. It's true.

There are dolphins at the aquarium too, and there are trainers that know everything about dolphins. There is also a lot of whistle blowing. The trainers blow the whistles and the dolphins listen and either come to the trainer or do back flips and other tricks.

When you're at the Shedd Aquarium, you'll hear a lot of splashing around in the water. And the whole place smells fishy from the trainers feeding the dolphins treats.   —*Andy Bautista, grade 4*

BOTH UGLY *and* PRETTY FISH

ONE TIME, my aunt took my sisters, my cousins, and I to the Shedd Aquarium. When we first got there, we had a picnic together. Then we went to see the dolphin show. The dolphins did flips and jumps. It was great because they could do them all at the same time.

The Shedd Aquarium also has lots of other fishes. There were ugly fish with big eyes and bumps all over their bodies. They swam slowly. There were also pretty fish with scales that were shiny like my favorite silver bracelet. There were lots of turtles. Some had hard shells as big as my desk at school! The plants with the fishes were orange and other colors and had tiny fish hiding in them.

When I got home, I dreamed that I was swimming with lots of fishes around me. Some were very big and some were really, really small. They were colorful and they wanted me to swim with them.   —*Mahnoor Syed, grade 4*

A MUST-SEE THAT YOU MUST SEE

THE SHEDD AQUARIUM is one of the must-sees you must see if you come to Chicago. They have lots of unique animals such as starfish, sharks, manta rays, dolphins, sea horses, beluga whales, Komodo dragons, sea lions, and otters. The newest animals are the Komodo dragons that came out not so long ago.

When I went to the Shedd Aquarium, I went to the wild reef. In the wild reef there are ocean fish like sharks and manta rays with other giant fish. I saw a great white shark there, which is the only shark that mistakes humans for fish and then attacks them. The first year I went to the aquarium I saw sea horses. They're kind of like kangaroos, only much smaller, and they have pouches to hold their young. The Shedd remodels that area near the dolphin show every year so it is different every time you go. Right after the sea horses it was starfish.

After you leave the Shedd, you may visit other museums since it's on the museum campus. Other museums like the Field Museum and the Planetarium are just minutes away. Parking is hard because many people come and enjoy seeing these marine animals.

—*Charles Lyang, grade 6*

FISH *from* MANY DIFFERENT OCEANS

THE SHEDD AQUARIUM is really cool. You can find a bunch of fish, sharks, lizards, dolphins, beluga whales, and sea otters. They also had something new called the coral reef. My parents paid twenty-seven dollars to go in and visit the coral reef.

When we went inside it smelled like salted water. I wore comfortable clothes like a t-shirt and jeans and sneakers. When I went to the coral reef I saw an Anglerfish. An Anglerfish is a fish that lives in Australia and different oceans. It camouflages itself on the ocean bottom and some of the Anglerfish like dark places. I even saw sharks there, too. There were six sharks in the tank. Some of the sharks included a bull and a tiger shark.

When you first come in the Shedd Aquarium you see a diver in the tank explaining all about the different fish in the tank. The diver was giving the fish lettuce. The little Hammerhead sharks enjoyed nibbling on that lettuce. The lizard house at the Shedd Aquarium was my favorite part. It had a spike lizard, a lizard called a Gila Monster, and a big lizard called a Komodo dragon, which I liked so much because it is very big and uses its tongue like a snake. The Komodo dragon also has poisonous breath when it hisses when it's angry.

If you're going to the Shedd Aquarium, it is best to go during the week because there are less people. You can even bring your relatives there. I went with my mom and dad. They went as a treat for me. —*Anthony Alvaladero, grade 5*

2 | dining out

WOULD GO BACK *in a* HEARTBEAT

THE MOST EXTRAORDINARY restaurant in Chicago is Athena Restaurant. It is in Greek Town in the South Loop. When we went there we didn't have to wait in line and the waiters were so nice. Athena Restaurant is in a red building and does not have any tables outside, but they make up for it with the beautiful scenery. There are flowers on the outside of the building, and inside they have posters and more flowers painted on the wall. I didn't really like the music they were playing, but that didn't matter because the food was so excellent.

Athena was really convenient for me and my friends. I say that because I am only thirteen and when I went one Sunday with my friends, nobody gave us any grief! And the food! The food was unbelievable! Not only that, but it was so cheap! I had a gyros with fries and drink, which came with free refills. It wasn't my first gyros, but it was the best!

Athena, in my opinion, is the greatest Greek restaurant. (I swear, I recommend it to everybody.) I love how if it is your birthday, they will sing songs for you and give you a birthday cake. While we were there, it was someone else's birthday and they sang to her. Three or four people stood around her table and sang, and they gave her a free cake.

If you love Greek food, you should really try Athena Restaurant. It is a lovely and beautiful family restaurant and I would go back in a heartbeat. I recommend Athena Restaurant to everyone, friends, and family. Writing this essay makes me want to go back and eat some more—soon!   —*Nicholas Tovar, grade 6*

VERY COLD DRINKS
with a LOT *of* ICE

BELLA'S PIZZA IS a great place to go. Do you know why? It is about two or one blocks away from my house and sometimes it makes the air smell like many different kinds of food. Bella's has the best, best food I have ever had. Specifically, you can get very cold drinks with a lot of ice in them. I really like that Bella's puts so much ice in their cold drinks. Bella's also has delicious pizza and they have comfy seats that make me feel like it is time for me to go to sleep.

One of my favorite times when I went there was when I got to be there on the half day of school. I went with my family. I got to eat pizza, nachos, and all my favorite food. We were celebrating that we got good grades on our report cards.   —*Melissa Delgado, grade 4*

A FOUNTAIN FULL *of* FISHES

THE BEST DAY I think I have ever had was when I went to Buffet City with my aunt and family. When I entered Buffet City, I saw a fountain full of fishes—including a catfish! Also, Buffet City had a rare display ship. It was nicely put on the counter with a Japanese flag on it. At the top of the fountain there was a diamond chandelier!

When I started picking food it made me hungry. It made my stomach growl—RRRRR! I chose a delicious-looking egg roll, some fries and ketchup, pizza, and some purple grapes. They also had ice cream and sushi.

Buffet City looks good inside. Their chairs were colored light brown and were waxed a lot. And if you need to go to the bathroom, I should tell you that they are nice. The bathrooms had wonderful grey tiles and the sinks and toilets were really shiny.

—*Josue Portillo, grade 4*

When you come to Chicago if you are starving, don't panic!

—*Karen Gaytan, grade 3*

YOUR MOUTH WILL DRIP SALIVA

ONE TIME I went with my family to Burrito Bowl. I would like to tell you where it is but my mom said it's a secret. One time I went, the people who work there put us in a table in less than five seconds. When I sat down the chairs were so comfortable. They were made up of 100% cotton. Then they gave us the menu. I ordered a burrito of beans. My sister ordered a torta of beef. My dad ordered three tacos and my mom ordered some beef with soup and a little guacamole. When the man came for the menu he asked us what we would like to order and my sister told him. In less than four minutes we were served already. We started to eat. It was so delicious it made my mouth drip saliva.

When I finished eating they said, "You are going to get three free tortas." We told them thank you. They also said, "And you get the food you ate for free." "This is because you guys come every day and we feel like your kids' uncles," they told us. When we left we called the rest of our family and told them to go. It was the best day ever.   —*Jaime Garcia, grade 5*

A WONDERFULLY HEALTHY BOWL *of* FUN

EDO SUSHI IS the ultimate Asian experience in Chicago nightlife. They have excellent sushi, according to my sister Stella, and they have a killer Korean dish called Be Bim Bop. Packed with an egg, rice, lettuce, an assortment of greens, an option of beef, hot sauce, and pickled cucumbers, Be Bim Bop is an amazingly delicious and wonderfully healthy bowl of fun. They also have a delicious dessert called mochi that is rice paste with ice cream in the middle. I get it for dessert every time I come because it ties together a delicious Asian cuisine. Even better is the Japanese Ramune soda, available in bubble gum and citrus flavors. Ramune is a refreshingly delicious soda that will really satisfy your sweet tooth.

On the last day of the ISAT, a test that all Chicago students take, we had a celebratory dinner at Edo Sushi. Even though I was the only one that ordered Be Bim Bop, we all enjoyed it very much. The sushi chef eagerly stood at the sushi bar waiting to make the sushi that my family ordered. My sister loves the salmon sushi, so the owner brought out this brand new salmon sushi, straight from Japan.

Edo Sushi is one of the only places in Lincoln Park that has Be Bim Bop and I take all my relatives to Edo Sushi. I recommend it to anyone eager for a taste of Asian. The staff makes you feel like family, and there is even a DJ on Saturday nights! There is no doubt about it, Edo Sushi is the best! —*Henry Barrett, grade 4*

MANY PEOPLE *and* DOLLS HAVE VISITED

GINO'S PIZZA IS the best pizza in the whole world. You can see the big crowd waiting for great food, and you can see all the writing on the walls and chairs. It is a place where people of all ages can come, relax, and eat some delicious pizza. Also, it looks kind of scary. I imagine it like a place where rock bands like Green Day or Good Charlotte would play. When you go to the bathroom you see all these pictures of people and dolls that have been there, like Chuckie and his wife, Usher, The Black Eyed Peas, and many more.

I will also never forget the first time I went there. A week before we went, my tooth was loose. I was brushing my teeth at my house and I felt something move. I looked in the mirror and I saw my tooth was loose but left it in. Then we were at Gino's and my mom said, "Eat a breadstick!" I don't like breadsticks, so I said "No!" Then I bent over to get another slice of pizza and, just then, my mom popped a breadstick in my mouth and I bit it. When I looked at the breadstick, there was my tooth! Everybody was amazed and they started laughing. I also started laughing. After everyone stopped, I tried to take a bite of another slice of pizza, but the pepperoni fell on the floor and when I bent down to get the pepperoni I dropped the whole slice on my shirt!　—*Rosendo Mentado, grade 5*

If you get Giordano's stuffed pizza, I hope you like cheese because there's pretty much a lot of it.

—Angel Guevara, grade 3

A PIZZA CRUST
THAT'S HUMONGOUS

MY FAVORITE PLACE to eat pizza is at Giordano's. Giordano's is a small place, but delicious. It has booths and regular tables too. I prefer eating in a booth because the chairs are soft and it is much more comfortable.

One of my favorite appetizers is the mozzarella cheese sticks. I like them because they are crunchy and not that hard to chew. Also, when you eat the cheese sticks, you can feel the grease go through your teeth. You could eat the cheese sticks plain, or you can dip them in marinara sauce. A vegetable they have that's delicious is the deep-fried zucchini sticks. They are really crunchy. You can also put marinara sauce on it, just like the cheese sticks.

For pizza, I recommend the stuffed pizza because it is really thick. The pizza's crust is humongous! You have a choice of pepperoni or sausage. Inside the pizza, there is pepperoni, sausage or whatever you like. There is also a lot of cheese. On top of the pizza, there is tomato sauce. A kid my age could probably eat one or two slices. My dad eats three.

There are many drinks like water, Coca-Cola, 7Up, and more. When you go to Giordano's, you should look appropriate and nice. You can wear jeans, but you have to wear something that matches. You should have manners and be polite. But if you are just going to pick up food, you don't have to look nice at all. Those people are usually wearing sweat pants.

Giordano's is a place that I always recommend for people to eat. I enjoy the food there and have fun with my family.

—*Marcus Yee, grade 5*

RED CURTAINS *and* MERMAIDS

A SUNDAY AFTERNOON HOTDOG MEAL

YOU SHOULD GO to Giordano's because they have great food. They have delicious, cheesy, stuffed pizza. It's a little bit fancy because it has red curtains, mermaids on the walls, and clean tables.

I went one day when it was my mom's birthday. We went with my aunt and cousins, and we ate pizza and cheese sticks. We sang "Happy Birthday" and I think my mom felt happy. Then we ate a little bit of cupcakes. The waitress was nice and she left us lollipops. Later on, we opened presents at home.

When you get to Giordano's, order the stuffed pizza. It comes with cheese (lots of cheese) and tomato. With the stuffed pizza, getting anything else is just too much. Except for a Sprite. You should have that to drink. —*Antonio Morales, grade 3*

illustration by Andres Zavala, grade 3

A SPICY WING DIPPED *in* SPICE

I LIKE SPICY WINGS from a place called Golden Fish and Chicken near Brownell School. When we approach the restaurant, I smell that delicious spicy chicken and my mouth gets watery.

The way they make it is simple. They slap on some flour with the seasonings and dip it in. It tastes crispy and fresh. I especially like the seasonings on the chicken wings, which are salt, pepper, and spicy sauce. I eat them with fries and the sauces I prefer are ranch and mild sauce. The mild sauce is still spicy. I like to eat the chicken with my dad because he likes the same sauces. We choose the same sauces in every season, all year, winter and summer.

I like to go to Fish and Chicken at least every three weeks so that I can smell like a spicy wing dipped in spice!

—*Justin Mathews, grade 5*

YES, IT IS DELICIOUS!

EVERY ONCE IN a while me and my family go to Grandma Sally's. It is on North Avenue near the Sears and the gas station. When I'm there I get a meat omelet. It has eggs, hash brown potatoes, sausage, bacon, and cheese. Yes, it is delicious!

We like to go there mostly on Saturdays and Sundays. It is really very crowded. We have a certain booth we sit in that is by the window. I just love that seat. When we sit down, we sit with parents on one side and kids on the other.

Most of the time when I go I see people from my school that are my friends. Sometimes I ask my parents if I can sit with my friends after we all finish our meals. They say "Sure!" Sometimes after I'm with my friends I ask my parents, "May I go over to Marion's house?" or "May I go over to Darlene's house?" They say that they'll talk to my friend's mother or father and then they usually say "Sure!"

I remember one time when Grandma Sally's was very crowded and we were waiting in line. My friend Marion was in line in back of us with her family. I couldn't believe what happened: we all sat together at the same table! I was kind of mad because we were at a table instead of my favorite booth but it was pretty fun to sit with my friend because it was summer and I hadn't seen her in a while. —*Brittany Burrell, grade 5*

YOU CAN SMELL *the* CHICKEN COOKING

WHEN YOU GO to Hoe Toy Chop Suey, you should order chicken. Sometimes it takes a long time for the chicken to cook. Those times you can actually smell the chicken cooking. If they have already cooked the chicken, it won't take as long. You can also order chicken over the phone. That is easy, but you still have to drive to get your order. Prices are mostly five and six dollars.

At Hoe Toy, they give you fortune cookies. You can order single fortune cookies or a whole bag. My fortune once said, "If you think about purple all week, good luck will come to you." I want a fortune that would say, "Your parents will get you a dog."
—*Autumn Evins, grade 3*

DELICIOUS *and* AMAZING GRITS

JOE'S HAS THE BEST french toast and the best grits. Joe's is located on the South Side of Chicago and they make the french toast whichever way you like it. I like my french toast well-done and with powdered sugar. They also have delicious and amazing grits and bacon. When they serve the food they make sure that they prepare it just the way you like it. If you don't eat pork, beef, or any type of meat, they have the best veggie sausages, and all types of vegetables and fruit.

I go to Joe's with my grandma, mother, and my daddy. If you have an early morning birthday party, they will sing an entertaining song. The birthday song is creative and they will give you a free cake or cupcake. If it were my birthday, I'd want a chocolate cake with strawberries.

If you're a regular customer, Joe's will give you discount sometimes and sometimes they'll take something off of the bill. Joe's is a small restaurant but they have beautiful paintings and it is designed to make you feel welcome. I feel welcome every time I go, and I am sure you will too.   —*Myliah Terry, grade 6*

Nicky's has good food and you will know Nicky's because it looks like the old days.

— *Kevin Hernandez Cortez, grade 3*

LIKE NOTHING YOU HAVE TRIED

MAMA LUNA'S, on Cicero and Fullerton, is a beautiful restaurant with candles, white tablecloths, and delicious smells. Mama Luna's is also pretty quiet.

You have to go to Mama Luna's because they have the best pizza you have ever tried. The cheese on the pizza is moist and hot. It will burn your tongue and taste so good that you will want to eat the cheese only and not the pizza. The crust is so delicious and I advise you to get thin crust because it is so soft. The best part of the pizza is the sausage because it tastes like pork. If you like pork, you'll like sausage.

Now let's get to Mama Luna's spaghetti. It is delicious and the meatballs are so good. The sauce that they use is like nothing you have tried. I like to eat the pasta regular, without meatballs, and then sometimes with meatballs. If I were you, I would eat the pizza the first time you go and next time I would eat the spaghetti.

Last year, my mom took me and my cousin there. It was my birthday. When we got to the restaurant, I saw that everyone from my family was there. It was a surprise party! We all had pizza and laughed a lot.

Mama Luna's—you have to try it. —*Jennixhia Rodriguez, grade 5*

THEY DON'T JUST HEAT IT UP

MON LUNG IS on Ashland Avenue and it just has the best Chinese food. They have a variety of different food, like shrimp lo mein, won ton soup, egg rolls, shrimp fried rice, and crab rangoon. They don't use too much grease either. They use a medium amount of grease because if they use too much it loses its flavor. Another thing that is good about Mon Lung is that when you order food it doesn't come fast. It comes slow. And what I like about it is that they make their food from scratch. They don't just heat it up and serve it to you. All their food is good so you should go visit this delicious Chinese restaurant.

I have known Mon Lung for as long as I can remember. I knew it when I was small. When you go to Mon Lung they have very nice waiters. They're polite and say, "Have a good day!" They give you fortune cookies, too. Now there is a new part of Mon Lung. They made a second floor so that it can fit even more people. I can't remember exactly what color it is painted but I think it is white. Mon Lung has very nice things around it like colorful lamps that make it moody.   —*Norma Sance, grade 5*

illustration by Eduardo Perez, grade 4

A SATURDAY BANANA SPLIT

ON SATURDAY MORNINGS, usually after an episode of Sponge Bob or The Simpsons, I take a walk to buy ice cream. My two-year-old brother waits at home while I walk. He knows I'm going to get ice cream but knows he won't get any.

While I walk down Greenview, I see cars racing. There's a big yard where my friends play soccer and flag football, but I pass this fun for a tasty treat at the Oberweis store on Milwaukee Avenue. My favorite is the banana spilt, with M&Ms, and sprinkles on it.

Once I get my treat I bring it home and hide it from my brother. He thinks I maybe put it in my backpack or under my shirt, but I hide it on a windowsill until he leaves and eat it while watching more TV.

Until my birthday party last week things were this way. At my party there were at least twenty people. I got many gifts and some money. My big cousin Jose busted the Chivas piñata with a long metal pole. He looked funny as he swung at the piñata. When he broke it candy spilled and everyone grabbed as much as they could.

Now that I have money from my party, I have bought my brother ice cream. I keep my money in a blue box under my bed. I took ten dollars from the box and bought Frostbites, my brother's favorite flavor. We were both happy.   —*Jonathan Rivas, grade 4*

A COLORFUL PIG WILL GREET YOU

IF YOU GO to Ocean Buffet you will see a colorful pig on the cash register. Once you register, you will be able to go and pick out your food. You don't have to worry if you finished your food and you're still hungry because you can have as many plates as you want. And don't be concerned about your money, because you pay to get in, not for the plates you eat. Ocean Buffet has ham rolled up with a hot dog, and they have plenty of snacks like fortune cookies, pudding, and Cheetos. You can pick whatever combination of food you want. My favorite combination is the macaroni with pizza and Texas toast.   —*Adriana Davis, grade 3*

TASTY FOOD, GOOD SERVICE, *and* CAKE

YOU SHOULD EAT at Portillo's because it is a special place to take your family. You can enjoy all the tasty food, the good service, and their cake. What I like to get the most is the hot dog, because it is so good. This juicy hot dog has peppers, tomatoes, onions, radish, a dash of black pepper, and a hot dog bun.

At Portillo's they have lots of lights and a jukebox that you can put coins in and play a song. You go to the stand to order and they give you a number. Then you can sit anywhere. When they call your number you walk up to the stand to get your food and then sit back down.

My mom and I last went to Portillo's three weeks ago. My mom drove her truck. She usually gets Italian beef with peppers. She orders extra meat but with the normal amount of juice. That day I got cheese fries. They give you cheese either on top or on the side in a cup. That way you can dip your fries if you want.

I like going to Portillo's with my mom. We get to have fun. We sit down talking about the day. She tells me how good her day was and we talk about the plans we might have tomorrow or today.   —*Naja Harrington, grade 3*

When you go to Chicago, you should go to Stella's Diner. I used to go there. I can't even remember the last time I went there before I never went there again!

—Dylan Haddad, grade 6

IT'S TWIST-TWIST GOOD

WHEN YOU EAT at Red Robin's the chicken will make you holla! Their food is great. If you know the word "spectacular" then you know what their food tastes like. There is just one thing I eat there — cheese pizza. The pizza is twist-twist good. What I mean by twist-twist is how you have to move your head to get the cheese off of the pizza. I also like to have a chocolate shake there. My grandma brings whipped cream from home with her to put some extra on my shake. My sister doesn't like the cherry on her shake, so I take it and put it on mine.

One thing about Red Robin's is that they have a big scary chicken statue and its eyes follow you around. There might even be a camera inside of it. My sister, even though she is two, is not scared of the chicken. She tries to hug it! Then when she sees the games and toys at Red Robin's she forgets about the scary chicken!

One time I was at Red Robin's for my birthday. I was excited to get a cake there because the only thing I like about my birthday is the cake, the ice cream, and the presents. One of the waitresses was bringing the cake and everybody was singing and clapping their hands. But then my little sister took the string off of her balloon and threw a toy at it. The balloon went flying across the room. The waitress tried to dodge it, so she wouldn't get the balloon in her face, but then she tripped over a TV wire and my cake went flying across the room!

I didn't see any of this because I was keeping my eyes real close on the scary chicken. When I turned my head, I got cake on my face. I licked it off and said, "Mmmm…vanilla." When I was leaving I put a little bit of cake on the chicken. They said this was okay, though, because they messed up my cake.   —*Yasmin Jones, grade 3*

WILL HAVE YOU COMING EVERY DAY

IF YOU GET HUNGRY, you should go to Ruby Tuesday. It is a good place to eat and you can try new foods there. Some of the new food I tried was the Alfredo sauce. It tastes like cheese sauce but it is white cheese that comes on flat, long pasta. You can get a salad with chicken and lots of vegetables to go with it.

At Ruby Tuesday the food is so great that it will have you coming every day. And when it is your birthday, they bring you a cake after you eat. On my birthday, we had a chocolate cake that was better than any chocolate cakes I ever had! All of the waiters bring the cake to you and they all sing the "Happy Birthday" song.

The waiters at Ruby Tuesday are very responsible and careful with the food you're going to eat. The waiter we had had two plates in both of his hands. He held them above his head and was very careful when he put them on the table.

Also, at Ruby Tuesday there is a huge parking lot that goes all the way around the whole restaurant. Even in the front and the back! This is different from most parking lots at restaurants in Chicago. I can't wait until I can go back because Ruby Tuesday is the best restaurant I have ever been to.   —*Cesar Melendez, grade 3*

» TRANSLATION ON PAGE 231

SIENTO QUE ESTOY *en* LAS NUBES

HABÍA UNA VEZ que mi familia fue al restaurante El Salvador. Toda mi familia estaba feliz porque allí es muy grande y muy bonito. Si tu familia fuera a El Salvador estarían muy feliz. Gritarás allí porque es muy maravilloso. Decía a mi mamá que yo queiro tener una fiesta allí. Me gusta porque las esculturas y las plantas son muy bonitas. Muchas personas vienen a El Salvador y todavía todo es muy precioso. Yo siento que estoy en las nubes y yo pienso que las personas también piensen que están en las nubes. Toda la comida es muy rica. Tienen papusas, taquitos y tortas. El arroz, los frijoles, y la fruta son muy especiales. Las popusas que hacen son muy deliciosas. Toda mi familia está feliz en el restaurante El Salvador. Ojalá que una vez más familias pueden ir a comer allá.   —*Tattiana Camargo, grade 3*

FRIENDLY, FUN, *and* TASTY

SCOOTER'S, THE NUMBER ONE frozen custard stand store, is located on Paulina and Belmont. It has every style of custard you could think of. There are "concretes," which is frozen custard with mix-ins and flavorings of your choice. If you turn a concrete over, it won't fall out! There are also milkshakes, which are extra thick and you can put anything in them. Then there is this really cool thing called Flavor of the Day. All ice cream stores have vanilla and chocolate (BORING!) and so does Scooter's, but it always has a different flavor daily. Scooter's is friendly, fun, and tasty!

Once on a really, really hot day, me, my mom and my brother Joe were all pooped, so we decided to walk to Scooter's. My mom agreed to treat us to concretes. I got a really rich, tasty flavor: orange cream! The taste of orange cream is a mix between the sweet vanilla ice cream and the tartness of the orange. POW! My brother (genius) remembered the reputation of the concrete and turned it over to test it…SPLAT! It fell out on the ground. As I mentioned, it was really hot out! He never did it again.   —*Lizzie Walsh, grade 4*

If you're tuff, you could eat Mr. Thai's spicy noodles.

—*Andrew Mayen, grade 4*

NEAT *and* ORDERLY FOOD

LA SIERRA IS the city's best restaurant because the staff is so friendly and their food tastes great. My mom, my dad, and my four brothers usually go to La Sierra on Saturdays for lunch. When we go there to eat, the owner turns on the big plasma TV and gives us the remote to change the channel if we want. We usually flip to cartoons or Spanish soccer.

When we are all settled, the waiter comes to us and asks me in a kind way, "What do you want to eat today?" I always order eggs, rice, and ham. The food looks so great when it comes right out of the oven and from the stove. When the waiter serves it, he gently says, "Here you go." When I see the food, it looks delicious because it is all neat and in order and it smells so good.

When I pick up the food at La Sierra and put that food in my mouth, I feel the hot steam and I taste the juicy, hot egg and the orange rice. Since my mom is a friend of the owner, he says "Thank you. Come again." And when we leave he lets us choose a sucker of any kind. They all taste great but the cherry suckers are my favorite.

La Sierra is also a terrific place to go for special occasions like birthdays or holidays. My cousins and aunts and uncles come to celebrate special occasions with my family. La Sierra is such a good restaurant. There is always so much food to try. —*Ian Quiroz, grade 6*

A GOOD DATE PLACE

THE GREATEST RESTAURANT to go to in Chicago is Suparossa on Montrose and Fullerton. It has a bar side and a restaurant side with white tablecloths and lights hanging from the ceiling. There's a jukebox so that you can pick your own music. They bring fresh bread, olive oil, and Parmesan cheese to the table. They have homemade soups and salads. Great pasta.

The food is fresh and tasty. The waiters and waitresses are nice and check on you often. It is the number one place to go when you really want Italian food. During the day it is not too crowded. At night more people are there, mostly couples and families. It would be a good date place.

One winter night my dad and I went to Suparossa and had a fabulous time. My dad had the fettuccini Alfredo, which was fabulous, and I had their chicken soup. We both agree that if you want a great Italian meal, go to Suparossa.   —*Jenny Gonzales, grade 6*

NICELY DRESSED, FRIENDLY WAITRESSES

EL TACO VELOZ is a great place to go. It has good food like enchiladas, tortas, and tacos. My dad cooks the food and my aunt takes the orders. They are both managers. My mom knows many of the waitresses. The waitresses are nicely dressed and very friendly.

El Taco Veloz has delicious drinks like Sprite and orange soda. It also has jamaica, which is homemade and sweet and has no bubbles. Desserts are good there, too. They have cake, flan, and cherries as toppings for both. They play all kinds of music at El Taco Veloz, and they also have lots of colorful lights. The decorations there are nicely done during Christmas, Halloween, and Day of the Dead.   *—Ivonne Vasquez, grade 4*

illustration by Darla Alvarez, grade 4

GUARANTEED *to* LICK YOUR FINGERS

YOU NEED TO COME to El Taco Veloz, located at Chicago Avenue. This restaurant is special to me because I celebrated there when I did my first communion. My family likes to go there for special occasions. Sometimes if it is your birthday, they will sing you a song honoring your birthday.

We know the people that work there. My mom knows the owner's wife because she goes to our church. She is very friendly and nice. The waiters are all really helpful and know a lot about the food. They will help you find food that you will like.

My favorite food is the steak tacos. The steak is really tasty and juicy. The tacos have cheese, lettuce, avocados, and other ingredients. The restaurant gives you hot sauce so you can put on as much as you want. I love their shrimp soup when it is cold outside because it really warms you up.

There is so much more food at El Taco Veloz that is so delicious. I guarantee that you will lick your fingers. I have been to Mexico twice and Mr. Taco Veloz is just like something you might find in Mexico. So, go go! Don't walk! Run to El Taco Veloz!
—*Selena Rivera, grade 5*

THE BEST DAY EVER

THE BEST RESTAURANT in Chicago is Amigo Chino! It has the most delicious food and it doesn't cost much. The food there is Mexican. I am 50% Mexican and 50% American and I love eating the food from where my family is from. I thought Amigo Chino would be Chinese because the name means "The Chinese Friend" but it isn't.

Amigo Chino is a small place. The people who work there are really nice people and they like to talk to you. On very special holidays they decorate the place really nice. They serve the most delicious Mexican food and have huge plates, the biggest you have ever seen. And they have great desserts too!

My best memory was the first time I went there. They gave a free piece of cake to everyone. That day I found a dollar on my chair! And a toy! I was so happy! I then had delicious soup with shrimp. It was so good! I ate so much and came home with the biggest stomachache of my life. That was the best day ever.

I hope that you remember to go to Amigo Chino. It is the best restaurant around. It is at the corner of Irving Park and Central. If you can't find it, look for the white sign with a man who cooks on it, and the name Amigo Chino on top! —*Aurora Correa, grade 4*

BLASTED *by the* SMELL *of* GREAT FOOD

MY DAD HAS PERFORMED at the Wild Hare Reggae Club many times and has won trophies from the government of Chicago. My dad has a band there and they all live in Chicago. He lives in the suburbs and comes to pick me up sometimes to take me to the Wild Hare to eat African food. They say the Wild Hare is all about good food and good music. It is very true.

The smells that come from the kitchen at the Wild Hare are amazing. They make the food in the back but the smell travels through vents and through open doors. It is a nice building to see and, when you go in, you are blasted by the great smell of the food. The Wild Hare is crowded on game nights because people watch the games there on the TVs. I love watching my dad and other singers perform there, and I get to eat delicious food!

When I am at the Wild Hare I eat this one African food called fufu. There is meat and bread in fufu. Sometimes in the American version they put broccoli on the side. You can add hot sauce, but you don't really need it because it's already really spicy. You can drink pop or water with fufu. The Wild Hare also has pizza—pepperoni, cheese, or sausage. I prefer to eat the fufu, though, because it tastes great and there are only three or four restaurants in Chicago that have fufu.

I should also say that they have great music at the Wild Hare. The dancing is great, and they put the music on, and you just got to grooooove.   —*Samuel Ghansah, grade 4*

3 | *dining in*

THE BEST *on the* CONTINENT

IN MY OPINION, my mom makes the best cheesecake in North and South America. It is the best cheesecake I have ever tasted and I think it is the best cheesecake I will ever taste. Every person in my family makes cheesecake, but I like my mom's the best.

The first time I had my mom's cheesecake, I was five years old. It was spring and we ate it after church. The cheesecake came after a big meal of string beans, macaroni and cheese, and fried chicken. She surprised us with the cheesecake and I didn't know what it was.

Now I know when my mom is making cheesecake. I can smell the crust cooking in the oven and hear the blender blending. I like to taste the leftovers that are in the bowl, see the cheesecake in the refrigerator, and touch the pan at the dinner table. My mom makes her cheesecakes in different ways. Some of them have crust on top and some have swirls. She also makes some that are caramel cheesecake, chocolate cheesecake and my favorite—the original cheesecake. The original cheesecake is the best because it is way creamy. She makes it on special occasions like Christmas, the Fourth of July, and also Easter.   —*Boyé McCarthy, grade 5*

My dad's lemon cheese-cake tastes like you're in a bubble of miracle.

—*Nadeja Holloway, grade 3*

BETTER THAN *a* RESTAURANT'S

MY MOM'S MACARONI and cheese is better than a restaurant's. I like many things about her macaroni and cheese, especially how it smells and tastes. Macaroni and cheese helps me to get strong and run faster.

Once on my birthday I went to a Chinese restaurant near my house. Me and my family ate macaroni and cheese there. It was not as good as when my mom makes it though. When she makes it, she will buy the macaroni, open the box and then cook it for twenty minutes. Then she puts the cheese into the macaroni and will mix it for ten seconds before I eat it. Macaroni and cheese is something you should eat almost every day because it is just so tasty and so good. I try to eat it about three times per week. —*Carlos Botello, grade 3*

illustration by Kathy Hernandez, grade 2

FAR AWAY, BUT WORTH IT

MY AUNT MAKES the best tamales. Even though she lives far away, and we have to drive on the expressway to get there, I still go to her house every other Sunday to see her and eat her tamales. When I go there, I can smell the meat coming from the stove as soon as I walk in. Her whole house smells delicious, and sometimes my aunt lets me have a taste before they're ready.

Sometimes I watch her making the tamales so I know what she puts in them. She uses cheese, beef, meat, chicken, sugar, peppers, mushrooms, red sauce, and green sauce. When she is finished making them, she puts them on a plate, and then she gives us a Coke. Finally we get a napkin, fork, and a knife, and we're ready to eat the tamales. My favorite taste is the green sauce mixed with the meat. Mmm, sabroso! Mmmm good! Go tamales!

—*Jimena Razo, grade 3*

FOR FAMOUS PEOPLE ONLY

MY FAMOUS CHOCOLATE CHIP COOKIES are for famous people only because of their creamy goodness. Famous singers, rock stars, and dancers eat these creamy cookies. I know famous people eat them because they're so sprinkly.

We buy the famous cookie dough at Wal-Mart. It comes wrapped in a hard plastic container. We keep it in the refrigerator at our house. When I make the cookies I get the dough out and I make it into circles on my cookie pan, which is made of pottery. I can do this all by myself because my grandmother taught me how to make them. I sprinkle the chocolate chips all over the cookies, then I bake them for a half hour.

When the cookies come out of the oven the chocolate has melted, and the cookies are now creamy. You can put one in your hand and eat it now. The best way to eat it is by dipping it into a glass of milk.

If I get an A+ on my math test my mom says I can make my famous cookies. This happens a lot, because I am good at times.

—Jose Gatica, grade 3

My grandma makes the best pound cake. Her pound cake is brown and the size of a laptop.

—Dale Kendrick, grade 5

» TRANSLATION ON PAGE 232

LOS HACEMOS JUNTOS

MI MAMÁ HACE los tamales muy sabrosos. A veces mi mamá no puede hacer sola tamales y le ayudo para que no se canse haciendo tamales. Yo paso las hojas para hace tamales. A toda mi familia, incluyendo mis tíos, primos y hermanos, les gusta como mi mama y yo hacemos los tamales. Hacemos tamales sólo para fiestas como cumpleaños. Siempre que hacemos tamales mis tíos y primos dicen que son ricos. A mi mamá le gustan los tamales como yo. En los tamales hay masa, pollo, salsa de carne, y eso hace que sepan especiales los tamales. Mi mamá hace los tamales con las manos o a veces con algunos cubiertos como tenedor, cuchara, y cuchillos para cortar la carne. Los tamales me gustan porque mi mamá los hace verdecitos o dulces. Dulces tiene sabor y los verdes son un poquito verde y blanco. Me gusta hacer los tamales con mi mamá porque los hacemos juntos. Si están buscando mi mamá y yo es posible que pueden encontrarnos en la cocina haciendo tamales ricos para los cumpleaños de mi familia.   —*Yanet Morales, grade 4*

NEVER SQUISHY *or* SQUASHED

MY BROTHERS AND SISTERS and I are from Chicago but our parents are from Mexico. My mom knows how to make the best food and definitely the best tamales you'll ever eat. Her corn tamales smell soft, kind of like bread. The skin is soft like a roll of paper and kind of bumpy. In the middle the tamale is fat because that is the shape of the tamale. We usually put the tamale in the oven or on the stove to cook. When it is on the stove the corn burns but nothing on the inside burns. When they are ready, you put the tamale on your plate and wait two minutes. After two minutes, you can open the skin and eat it.

The inside of the tamale is sometimes chicken and sometimes just corn. I went with my dad one time and we bought tamales at the store. At the store you can order whatever kind of tamale you want, either with the red spice or the green spice. Sometimes the ones in the store are squishy and squashed. My mom's tamales are never that way. That's why I like them best.

If you don't have any tamales now, don't worry, I have them. Come on, hurry up! I can smell them cooking!   —*Luis Blancas, grade 3*

NOT MOST PEOPLE'S KIND *of* FOOD

MY FAVORITE FOOD is shrimp. My mom makes it every Sunday. It's a tradition. She sometimes cooks up crunchy, juicy, fried shrimp. It's so good. The shrimp is so gigantic and that's the best part. It fills us up for the whole night.

My mom buys the shrimp at a special store called One Stop. It's around the corner from my grandmother's house. The store is nice. It just got remodeled and painted. My cousin works there, so sometimes we see her when we are buying shrimp. When I eat shrimp, it somehow brings memories of my grandfather. He liked shrimp stew. I like shrimp stew too, but I take out the shrimp and eat the broth. I save the best for last, and eat all the shrimp after I've finished the broth.

We have different kinds of shrimp every Sunday. Sometimes my family comes over to have a shrimp feast and we talk and play. The grown-ups play cards, and usually all the kids play in my room. We watch television and play games. On special occasions my mom makes shrimp casserole and I add hot sauce to it. When she doesn't want to cook, she orders pizza with mushrooms, onions, olives, and shrimp. I pick everything off and eat the shrimp and pizza crust. My mom loves to cook and make different foods, but our two favorite dishes are garlic shrimp and shrimp fettuccine. We love this food because it's not most people's kind of food.

Shrimp is original. My advice to you is if you want shrimp fettuc-cine, gumbo shrimp, popcorn shrimp, and garlic shrimp come to my house! —*Krystal Giles, grade 5*

» TRANSLATION ON PAGE 233

UNA BOLA SUAVE QUE SABÍA DELICIOSO

FUE UN DÍA muy hermoso por el cumpleaños de mi mamá. Cumplió treinte y dos años. Mi papá pidió un pastel de chocolate. Llamamos a la casa de mi amiga. Llegaron y invite a brincar a la cama pero su mamá dijo que tuvieramos mucho cuidado que no nos caeramos. Después nos cansamos. Llegó el pastel y le cantamos las mañanitas. Tenía cuadros alrededor el pastel. Nos comimos pastel. Sentamos a que se nos bajara la comida. Pasaron quince minutos. Seguimos jugando tambien invite a mis vecinos llegaron. Mi mamá hizo posole en la madrugada. A dentro era maíz, tiene un puntito color café fuerte que eso le daba mucho sabor. Era una bola suave que sabía delicioso. Comimos posole huelía muy rico. Le dieron muchos regalos. A mi mamá los abró nos dijieron que fueramos abrir los regalos. Ella recibió un cuadro para fotos y dinero de mi papá. Los niños se fueron a su casa y recogimos la basura. Ví la tele y despúes sacudí la cama y me acosté a leer un cuento de los zapotos rojos hasta que me dormí. —*Elizabeth Tellez, grade 3*

» TRANSLATION ON PAGE 234

LA RECETA VIENE *a* CHICAGO *de* MÉXICO *de* MORELOS

CUANDO MI TÍA hace fiestas le dice a mi mamá que lleve el posole. Todas las fiestas tienen que ser en la casa de mi tía porque su casa tiene basement. Las demás de la familia tienen que traer comida. A mí me gusta cuando mi mamá le hace posole porque huele rico, sabe a maíz, a caldo, aguacate, tortillas chiquititas, huevo, limón, y lechuga o repollo. Cuando mi mamá hace posole yo le ayudo a descabesar el maíz y también le ayudo a ver al posole para que no se queme. A mí me gusta comerlo en días festivos como en cumpleaños, en Navidad y año nuevo. El posole huele a maiz y caldo y cuando es verano mi mamá lo hace el posole la casa se pone muy caliente. Mi mamá compra las cosas en la tienda La Petes. Creo que La Petes está en la calle Archer.

La receta de posole es de mi familia. Mi abuela también hizo el mismo posole. La receta viene a Chicago de México de Morelos, la parte de México donde viene mi familia. Mi familia está en los Estados Unidos para quince años y seguimos siempre haciendo el posole de mi abuela. —*Diana Benitez, grade 3*

TOO GOOD *for* TWO PERSONS

MY FAMILY'S SPAGHETTI is so powerful that you will never starve. It is the best spaghetti in the whole world! All of the people in my family are the best cooks of delicious spaghetti, especially my mom. Sometimes I eat spaghetti with my family, which is my mom, dad, and my best twin brother in the whole live world, Salvador. Every time I get an A+ or 100% on my math or reading test, my mom and I bake spaghetti together. We like to get funky with it. When we're cooking, we pretend to be rock-and-roll singers. We grab some cooking stuff like forks and spoons and start banging on the pot. (Once we broke a pot and the sauce ran out and we had to start again!)

Now I want to tell you some steps to make this terrific spaghetti. It is too good for two persons to eat it so you should have at least four people to enjoy the wonderful spaghetti. First, you cook the noodles for seven minutes. After the noodles are slimy, then you put the sauce on top of it. To eat it properly, you should use a fork to roll it into your mouth, or you could grab it with your hand, hold it above your head, and nibble it. It is going to be super slimy so be careful and grab it. Put it into your mouth and eat it! Yum, yum, yum, yum, yum, yum, yummy! —*Virginia Velarde, grade 3*

illustration by Elena Muro, grade 2

SHRIMP *from the* FUTURE

IF YOU WANT to eat some shrimp, you're welcome at The Shrimp House made by Donte Washington's mom. Come to The Shrimp House and you can eat all the shrimp you can ever dream of and any shrimp in the world! It's such a good restaurant that we can get some shrimp from the future, and you can make your own combo of shrimp, too. We are fast at cooking and cook the shrimp three different ways: fried, boiled, and baked. It is so good. The best kind of shrimp is seasoned with pepper, lemon pepper, and a little bit of salt. It tastes fantastic! The Shrimp House also has side dishes: potatoes, lobster, salad, and ten different kinds of soup.

The Shrimp House looks like other restaurants, but fancier. At The Shrimp House, we don't have waiting rooms because we have more tables than a restaurant has. When you first get to the table, it's all shiny, and while you are eating your shrimp you get a massage by a professional masseuse. When you are really, really, really hungry, you don't have to wait because in one second your meal will be right there. The waiters at The Shrimp House are all French, but they speak English and every other language too. French waiters are very fast! If you want some shrimp, you should come to The Shrimp House!   —*Donte Washington, grade 3*

WATCH THAT NOBODY STEALS IT

MY MOM BAKES the greatest chocolate ice cream cake in the city of Chicago. When she does it, she puts in all the ingredients—cake mix, eggs, and milk—into a big bowl and mixes them up. Then she puts it in the oven. I know when my mom bakes the chocolate ice cream cake because the whole house smells like chocolate. While I wait for the cake, sometimes I do my homework. Other times I take a shower, and when I come out the cake is ready. When the cake is finished baking, my mom puts in a lot of ice cream because she knows I love ice cream. When it is completely finished, I go to the table and eat it with my milk, always watching so that nobody steals my chocolate ice cream cake.

One time I didn't watch it enough. My little dog Princess is the kind of dog that never grows up, and she loves ice cream cake, too. One time I was eating and watching TV, and I went to the bathroom and left the cake on the couch. When I came back, there was no chocolate cake left and I felt so mad at her! I never want that to happen again, but I do like to share the cake with the friends in my neighborhood. So if you are ever in my neighborhood and want the greatest chocolate ice cream cake, just come to my house! —*Areli Nuñez, grade 3*

YOU'LL WANT ONE *or* TWO MORE

WHEN YOU COME down Prairie Street, you will say, "What's that smell?" That smell will be the delicious hamburger made by my father, Marieo Sr. I hope you do not miss it. It's so good it makes you want one or two more. The reason it's so good is because you'll find my dad using all these ingredients: onions, pickles, hot sauce, mayonnaise, ketchup, extra cheese, bread, mustard, and lettuce. He actually puts salt, pepper, and garlic inside the burgers. Mmmm. My favorite. If you ever get to have it, you won't ever want to get rid of it. Sometimes it tastes so fabulous you won't say anything at all, just "Mmmm…" over and over again. They're the bomb.

My dad always makes his special burgers on the Fourth of July, and we can see the neighborhood fireworks from our backyard. Sometimes we go to Navy Pier after we eat and watch the fireworks there, too. If it is a good, hot, summer day, my dad will make the burgers. He always grills in the backyard, and when I smell the burgers cooking I run into to the yard. Once, we had a big family cookout and the burgers were so good people took some home. If I was my dad, I would be so proud of myself that I would eat one burger myself before I gave one to everyone else.   —*Melissa Harvey, grade 5*

4 | *getting around*

LIKE RIDING *a* ROLLER COASTER

THE TRAIN IN CHICAGO is called the CTA. It has many different lines like the blue, red, green, and pink line. You should always be careful and make sure where you want to go. Looking at a map will help you see where you are going.

I like riding the train because it feels like I am riding a roller coaster, but I don't like it much when it gets very bumpy. When you are on a train, there are some things you shouldn't do. Make sure you don't stand up while the train is moving, open the door, be too loud, or make the conductor crash. And never step on the railroad tracks.

Sometimes my mom and I ride the blue line to pick up my grandma on the West Side. We take her where she needs to go and go back to her house with her.   —*Natalie Hernandez, grade 3*

FROM HYDE PARK *to* YOUR MOM'S HOUSE

IF YOU ARE GOING to take the train in Chicago, you can buy your ticket at the station, or your mom might have one. The train costs five dollars or twenty dollars and comes either in the early morning or at noon. You can take the train to many places including Hyde Park and your mom's house.

There are some rules to follow on the train: stay in your seat, don't open the doors, and stay away from the tracks until it is time to get on the train. When you ride the train, please don't bring your toys, food, or pets because people might have asthma.

Riding the train can be cheaper than a taxi because taxis cost more depending on how far you go. To go around the corner in a taxi only costs two dollars, but Texas might cost one hundred dollars, Puerto Rico five hundred dollars, and New Jersey about one million.   —*Rebeca Brito, Aesha Cano, Jabari Carroll, Nazir Davis, and Juan Jimenez, grade 2*

> To be a nice citizen, pull a lever for an old lady.
>
> —*Brenda Ramirez, grade 3*

> If you do not have money you should have walked.
>
> —*Jocelyne Luna, grade 3*

KEEP QUIET *and* JUST READ

SOMETIMES WHEN I'M on the train, I go up closer to where the conductor drives and I can see the tracks. I like it when the train goes fast, but sometimes I fall off my seat. I like seeing all the things around the train, like trees, buildings, streets, and birds. My sister and I make bets about the doors, like which side will open. I win a lot.

When you are on the train, do not distract the driver. There can be no eating on the train and no drinking on the train. Do not try standing on the train. Wear your seat belt, and don't throw the food that you are eating. It's a good idea to keep quiet and to just read. And I think you have to pay nineteen dollars to go on the train.

I had fun with my sister Kassandra, my brother Matthew, and my cousin Emilio when we took one train to the zoo and one train back with my godfather and his girlfriend. My brother Matthew likes to stand up a lot on the train, and I was telling him to sit down because I wanted to see out the window. My sister and I played "I Spy" games through the window and my sister won, but only half the time.   —*Vicky Cano, grade 3*

VERY SIMILAR *to the* INSIDE *of a* BUS

THE CTA TRAIN in Chicago is great to get around in because there are no cars or buses that can get in front of you when you're on it. Also, I like how the train drives fast so that people can get where they need to be on time. When the train goes underground, it sometimes scares me because of the loud sounds and sparks all over the tracks. But when we get back over the ground, I get happy.

I take the train when I am hungry. My daddy takes me in the afternoon, on weekends. We take the train because it's more fun than driving. We take the train to Cracker Barrel, Pizza Hut, and Baba's. We even like taking the train on the way home.

To find the CTA, you go down the stairs at the Roosevelt or Pulaski stops. There is a place where you can put your ticket and then you go through a turnaround that lets you in. When you get on the train you'll see that the inside of a train is very similar to a bus. I listen to music, read books, and write stories for Grandma on the train.   —*Jasmine Hines, grade 4*

GETTING AROUND

On the CTA, it can take me two minutes or two hours to get to my grandma's house.

—Danisha Greyer, grade 4

EXCITING THINGS CAN HAPPEN

MANY EXCITING THINGS can happen when you ride Chicago's trains!
I like to ride the blue and red lines. I take the train to Sox games
with my friends. On those days, the trains are crowded with White
Sox fans.

I always go on the train when my mom goes anywhere, especially downtown. There are parts of the ride that are exciting:
I like it when it gets dark and it gets very loud. It makes me feel
depressed, though, when people on the train litter and the workers have to clean up the mess. People should pick up their own
garbage.

Some things to remember are that one needs to be careful not
to step on the crack by the train. Also, when your stop is coming
get ready to get off or you'll miss it. Finally, if you want to change
seats, make sure the train is stopped or else you'll fall over.

—*Isabella Garduño, grade 3*

IMPORTANT *for* PEOPLE WITHOUT CARS

IN DOWNTOWN CHICAGO, you can find lots of taxis around, mostly near the big buildings. Taxis are important transportation vehicles in Chicago for people who don't have cars or any way to get around. Once I went in a taxi with my Granny to a restaurant to get crab legs, shrimp, and lobster tails.

It is good to ride in a taxi but sometimes the drivers are rude. I was in a cab once and the driver was on the phone. He was having a loud conversation and he missed some turns. My mom even called the taxi company to complain. We didn't feel safe then.

Just so you know, to get a taxi to come, you have to whistle or stick your hand out. In Chicago, the cost of the taxi depends on how far you want to go. Two blocks is about five dollars, and if you want to go three blocks, I think it is ten dollars. —*Kyetrel Glass, grade 4*

ROTTEN FISH, WET DOG, *and* FRESH FLOWERS

IN CHICAGO, taxi cabs have numbers on top and are yellow. Sometimes the lights in the back are broken and the tires are flat, but they're not that dangerous. A taxi ride costs ten or fifteen bucks or more. You need to pay a tip—ten or fifteen cents.

The drivers wear black and yellow hats, like police officers. There is a window in the middle because the driver may not like you, or want to listen to you talking. It is kind of dangerous to be a taxi driver. Once, the police were chasing someone who stole something and a taxi driver crashed into a pole because all the cars were driving too fast.

Inside the taxi, it is soft and cushy with black seats. A lot of times seatbelts are missing, but if you have a baby, they'll call a better taxi for you. A taxi can smell either like rotten fish, wet dog, or fresh flowers, and sometimes all three at the same time. When the taxi comes right from the store it smells only like fresh flowers.

You can call for a taxi, you can wave, or you can show it that it should stop for you with your palm. You can also get a taxi by pounding the air with your fist. If you want, you could even chase after the taxi, but you probably won't catch it because it has more energy than you.   —*Melodi Hoff, Joshua Serrano, and Malik Shaw, grade 2*

illustration by Danny Vigil, Jr., grade 2

GET WHERE YOU'RE GOING FAST

ONE WAY TO GET AROUND the city of Chicago is by taxi cab, but you have to make sure when you get in that the taxi driver doesn't take all of your money. If you are going in a taxi for the first time, then make sure you are nice to the driver because he or she can kick you out if you are mean. Sometimes the taxi might smell nice, but of ten they can be smelly. Most taxis are yellow, but not all of them.

I took my first ever ride in a taxi cab when I was four years old. My mom was going to have a baby girl and we needed to get her to the hospital fast, so my dad called a taxi cab. When I got in, the cab smelled a little, and I was scared, but my family was with me, and I was excited. I remember the driver smiled at me and I started to feel better. When we got to the hospital my little sister was born, and she was so pretty!   —*Jasmin Jimenez, grade 3*

GOOD *for* SHORT RIDES *and* LONG RIDES

LET ME TELL you what I know about being in a taxi in Chicago. To get a taxi to pick you up, first you must go to a sidewalk. To let a taxi know that you need it, hold up two fingers and yell "Taxi!" (You wouldn't want to do this in your house, though. That's silly.) When you get in, the driver will ask you, "What kind of ride do you want? Short or long?" After you answer him, he'll tell you the amount of money you need to pay for the ride.

Before you get in the taxi, you must know the rules. First, there will be no pets allowed and certainly no eating or drinking. And never disturb the driver. Next, you must not shout in the taxi. And to be safe, make sure the kids stay seated in the back and that adults are seated in the front. Most importantly, stay in your seat with your seatbelts on. Stay comfortable!

Once, me and my family wanted to take a taxi cab. We were heading to Sears because we needed new stuff to fit in our house. We found ourselves a taxi in the middle of the street. Once we opened the door, the driver said we must pay him $7.50 because we were taking a long ride. Inside, there were blankets, pillows, and a DVD player. Behind the seats there were pockets. The only thing that was wrong was that, in the cab, there were no curtains to cover up the windows, which I didn't like because the sun hit me. Being in the taxi that day was like living at the beach! It was too hot!   —*Mario Diaz, grade 3*

DON'T FORGET *to* PAY *the* DRIVER

WHEN YOU TAKE a taxi, the first thing you do is get into the taxi. The second thing is to tell them where you want to go. To be safe you should put on your seatbelt and should not play around because the driver might crash, you will get hurt, they will have to call the police, and you will be taken to the emergency hospital. When you get out of the taxi you have to pay the driver because if you don't they will call the police and you will be in jail for the whole day. I've seen that happen on the news.

I like to take a taxi to the dollar store with my mom and dad after school. My mom is the janitor at the store and we stay until 6:00. On Wednesday nights there is a family reading night and it's almost like a library. —*Mario Herrera, grade 3*

I love a train and want
to marry it because
it is cute and pretty.

—*Brandon Gniadek, grade 3*

TALK WITHOUT PEOPLE LOOKING *at* YOU

WHEN YOU NEED to get around Chicago, it is cheaper to go by car than by bus since in the bus you'll have to pay. I can listen to my headphones while I'm in the car without people getting mad. When I'm in the car, I can also talk without people looking at me. And on the bus, people are sometimes rude and are playing with their teeth, their mouths, and their heads.

One thing that is a pain about driving a car is that parking is a lot of hard work. Another side of driving a car that is trouble is that traffic can be really bad. One time, when we were going to my uncle's surprise twenty-sixth birthday party, the traffic was so bad that when we got to the party they were already eating cake and ice cream!

Even though there are some problems, I would still rather take a car in Chicago because the buses are usually slower since they have to make all of those stops.   —*D'asia Blackmon, grade 4*

THE WHOLE CITY REFLECTED
in the SILVER BEAN

ONE OF THE BEST things about getting around Chicago in a car is that you can look out the window the whole time. You can see the tall and short buildings, stores, and restaurants. In some buildings I can see the elevators going up and down. I also see people walking to work, or to the train. Some people are waiting on the bus. When we drive on Michigan Avenue, I can see the whole city reflected in the silver bean. At night, I can see the moon and the lights of Navy Pier.

The rules to drive around Chicago are that you have to have a driver's license and wear your seat belt. You also need gas and a steering wheel. My mom is a good driver because she doesn't go too fast. It's just her and me in the car and we listen to music and talk. We listen to hip-hop or gospel. My favorite place to go is over to my dad's house. He lives in one of the very tall buildings.

One thing that is frustrating is traffic. It happens when a lot of cars stop driving. You have to wait to get where you are going because the cars are stuck.

It's great riding in my mom's car because I see so many things in Chicago out of the window and I get to be with my mom. Also, when we're in the car, I know I'll get to see my dad soon.

—*Daija Jackson, grade 4*

illustration by Rosa Ochoa, grade 6

RIDE IT WHEN YOUR CAR GETS PEELED

LAST WINTER MY mom's car got bumped by another car and the back of the car got peeled. After that we took the CTA bus. People take the bus to go all kinds of places. We once even took two buses to get to an eye exam.

Sometimes people get tired of standing on the bus and they sit down. The bus is good to take with your dad if you are going to school and he is going to work. I don't like to take a late bus because I could be late for school and dad could be late for work.

The most important thing is to pay your two dollars. Also, you should never get out of control because you might be kicked out of the bus.   —*Melanie Rolon, grade 3*

You must not play with the vine that stops the bus.

—*Eduardo Delgado, grade 3*

SOMETIMES PEOPLE DO CRAZY THINGS

I OFTEN TAKE the 69th, 68th, or 71st Street buses. I go to home or to school on the bus and always ride with my sister and brother or my mom. Sometimes it's all of us. The way that you can pay or get a bus card is to go to the currency exchange. They give you a card that you'll put in the very front part of the bus. Sometimes people try not to pay by getting on the back of the bus.

When my family rides, we don't talk; we just sit quietly. I just listen to the driver talk about how you're supposed to act on the bus. There is no eating, drinking, or radio playing on any CTA vehicles. But sometimes people do some crazy things. One time, people were fighting because teenagers were hitting passengers on the back of the head and running off the bus. The bus driver got scared and tried to drive off and a lady's leg got stuck in the door. Another time, I was trying to get on the bus when there was a lot of snow and I fell back into the snow, which made my cousin laugh at me. And one other time a man poked out his tongue and bottom lip at me and some other boy on the bus. After seeing these crazy things, I think I should take a car! —*Daja Mullen, grade 4*

The CTA bus is fun to ride because you can look out the window and sometimes there are crazy things happening outside. Get on the bus!

—Shadell White, grade 4

A VOICE TALKING BY ITSELF

THE FIRST TIME I took the bus was about four or five months ago. Since I only have one kidney, I have to go to the hospital every year. Our car didn't work then, and we had to take the bus. It was a city bus that went along Fullerton Avenue. Since it was my first time, I saw doors opening by themselves and a voice talking by itself. I wondered what the back door was for so I asked my mom what the three doors were for. My mom said it was for big emergencies.

We got to the hospital, but I wondered how the bus knew where we had to go. I think it knew where to go either because my mom told it where to go, or because it only goes to one place. When we got to the hospital everything was okay.

To this day, I only remember going on the bus once. I hope my car breaks down again so I can ride the bus again.

—*David Renteria, grade 3*

5 | *parks*

A QUIET PARK *to* SIT *and* READ

BUFFALO PARK IS a microscopic park where a life was saved. Well, it's just small, not microscopic. Buffalo Park is just a quiet park to sit and read, or listen to the cars drive by and the birds chirp. It is located in Ravenswood Manor near the Chicago River.

Let me tell you a true story of what happened in Buffalo Park. One day in September, my mom and I were sitting in the sun room when we noticed our neighbor walking by. Her name is Elaine and she has dog named Zoey. Zoey is a Border collie. We saw Elaine and noticed she had two dogs with her that day. She had a black Labrador retriever with her, too. I was very curious.

I noticed Elaine walking up to our house. "Ding Dong" went the doorbell. I answered it. "Hi, Elaine! Hi Zoey! Hi puppy?!" I said. "Who's that other dog?" I asked Elaine. She said, "I found him in Buffalo Park." Elaine knew we had been looking for a dog for months. She let go of the dog and he raced into my house. She asked, "Is it okay if I come back tomorrow and get him?" She was going to come back because she wanted to see if the shelter would take the dog. My mom said, "We will just put up signs instead of calling the shelter."

The next day, my mom and I put up signs. We waited a few weeks and nobody claimed him. We got to keep him and we named him Chief. I still have my dog to his day. We found him in

2005, and now it's 2007.

I think Buffalo Park is a great place to be. There's not much to do but it's just nice to sit around and enjoy the view. We would have never found our dog if Elaine wasn't there. Also she could've chosen anyone in the city of Chicago or ever anyone in the state of Illinois. But she brought the dog to us. That's how I got my dog, Chief. —*Aleah Kraft, grade 4*

GET WET UNTIL 12:00 MIDNIGHT

COMMERCIAL PARK IS the best park in the city and you will never want to leave! You will see the fun right when you're walking close to it! It's true.

133

Commercial Park has many things. They have a baseball field where you can also play football, and people can cheer you on. If your little brothers and sisters aren't into sports, they can go and play on the playground. There is also an arcade where you can win money and candy. At Halloween time, people go to Commercial Park because the park has a Halloween party and everyone is invited. The summer is a good time too because you can go there and get wet until 12:00 midnight.

I have many memories of times at Commercial Park. One time, my best friend Isaiah, who transferred from a different school, met me there and we played football.

I also had my birthday party there one year. I will never forget the very first or the very last time I went to Commercial Park, and I really mean that. —*Eddie Calderon, grade 5*

SHAPED LIKE *a* BIG SPOT *of* PAINT

HANSON PARK IS shaped like a big spot of paint. The outside edge is wavy and there are gates all around it. Hanson Park is special and is a big space. You can buy food and drinks there. When I am there, sometimes I see friends. I like when we play soccer. The wind goes to your face and you can play for almost a day. You can drink water and the water is very fresh. There is a special indoor place where you can pay three dollars to play soccer. It is much better than other parks where you have to play in fields where there might be nasty water on the ground. The nets indoors are smaller, so you don't need a goalie and you can play with five people. When you are tired, there is a room to rest there. You can drink coffee. I like that place a lot.

One time I went to Hanson Park with my dad. That day a guy showed up with special water with vitamins, frozen sandwiches, chips, and fruit. He also had a grill to cook the sandwiches. I don't know how it worked without a plug. But after that day he was there every day at the time we went there, and was waiting for us to buy some food.   —*Nestor Ortiz, grade 5*

Humboldt Park is the best park in Chicago and in all the countries in the world.

—*Noe Villeda, grade 4*

THE PERFECT PLACE *for* *a* FAMILY PARTY

IF YOU GO to Humboldt Park, you will have a lot of fun, trust me. It's huge. It starts at California Street and ends at Kedzie. In the summer the grass is wet, green, and sometimes yellow. In the winter, it's cold and white. You can play softball, baseball, and kickball there. It also has a field where you can play basketball. It has a big pond where you can fish.

Humboldt Park is the perfect place to have a family party. I did. For my birthday, I couldn't go to Mississippi to see my family, so I asked my grandma if I could have a party at Humboldt Park. She said yeah. I invited my family and friends. I had a big cake. They put up a big sign that said "Happy Birthday". We played cards and had music. It was great.

Every year at the end of school, Humboldt Park has a big carnival. That carnival has popcorn, candy, and drinks. There is this ride that takes you upside down and another ride that goes back and forth really, really, really fast—like crazy. If you are like me, it will scare you. There is also a fun house where things pop you in your face. The fun house is scary but not as scary as the rides.

To really experience it, I recommend you go to Humboldt Park yourself!   —*Ayanna Bryant, grade 5*

illustration by Jacky Banda Leon, grade 5

FEELS LIKE IT NEVER ENDS

WHEN YOU COME to Chicago be sure not to miss Humboldt Park. It's a fun, big park, and it feels like it never ends.

Humboldt Park has a big pond. It also has a small beach, and you can go swimming. If you like fishing, you can go fishing there, too. There is a small playground that is filled with kids in the summer. If you're a basketball fan, they have basketball courts there. There's a field for playing catch, or playing with your dog, or playing baseball. There is just so much to do.

The Humboldt Park neighborhood is a beautiful Puerto Rican community, which means it has delicious food stands. On each side of the park there are stands selling Puerto Rican food like rice with beans and spices, papayas, and pear, mango and apple juices. My cousins come to Humboldt Park when the weather is nice and we walk around the park or ride our bikes.

Once I was in Humboldt Park when I was about ten years old, I leaned over the water to look in and dropped my basketball in the water. I tried to lean forward to get it out and fell in. When I got out I was wet, and I had sticks and seaweed in my hair and on my clothes. My mom and my brother laughed at me. Then, when my clothes dried, I smelled like wet dog.

If you ever come to Humboldt Park don't forget the pond, or the beach, or going fishing, or the playground, or the basketball court, or the field. And, last but not least, don't forget the delicious food stands! —*Jasmine Castillo, grade 6*

A GREAT PLACE *to* BUILD CASTLES

THE BEST PLACE in my neighborhood is Leone Park. It is right on Lake Michigan. Leone Park is one and one half blocks from my house. In the summer, my family goes about once a week. When you're there, you can play in the sand and build sand castles. It is really great for castle building.

You can also play in the freezing lake. When you get there, the water is always cold, but then you get used to it. Riding your bikes can be tiring but you can go in the lake and cool off. You can play basketball, football, and soccer. I like playing soccer in the sand with my friends, and swimming in the lakes. If you play football and soccer, some trees will block the sun's rays.

In summer, you can go to summer camp there, and sometimes there are campouts. Even if you're not in summer camp, you can still go camping. In summer camp, you can use little boats and surf boards, but you have to take a swimming test. You have to swim from the rocks to a bridge, then back, then to the bridge again. If you pass this test, you have to run a mile to warm up and then you jump in the lake. When you end up passing the whole test, you are allowed to ride in an inflatable tube while a boat pulls you.

Leone Park is my favorite place in my neighborhood. You can go on walks there and on summer nights you can hear the crickets playing their music.   —*Sebastian Jimenez, grade 6*

BOTH SIDES *of the* FORK ARE GOOD

ONE TIME, I went to a playground with my dad that was called Lerner Park. When you enter, you follow a path past a tennis court and then you'll see a fork in the road. One way takes you to a small ballpark and the other takes you to a playground. Both sides of the fork are good.

While we were there, we were sitting on a bench when all of the sudden me and my dad saw a skunk. Then, we saw a cat by a tree. We watched to see when the skunk would see the cat and when he did he was as curious as Curious George! The skunk raised his tail and went over to the cat and sprayed its nasty smell. We laughed and said, "Poor cat!" The cat hissed, ran away, and probably screamed.   —*Ariana Aprim, grade 3*

They put new lights in Kosciuszko Park so that people won't lose their balls around the time of nine.

—*Miguel Coria, grade 5*

YOU CAN MAKE MEMORIES

LINCOLN PARK IS a place where I can make new friends and play on the playground. It is pretty quiet and I like listening to the birds and even feeding them there. You can make memories there.

One of my favorite memories is of the day that my family played and hung out before summer break was over. My mom, my dad, my brother, my sister, and I all rode our bikes there together. My dad had the basket. We had a picnic with egg rolls and sandwiches and bananas for a snack. We got tired, so we all rested on the ground. Then my brother and sister played on the swing while I went down the slide. My mom and dad enjoyed the sunset together. Then when it was dark we rode our bikes home. My family really had a special time in Lincoln Park that day. *—Li Nguyen, grade 4*

143

PARKS

RELAXING *and* FUN *for the* KIDS

HAVE YOU EVER gone to McKinley Park? Well I have. It's an enormous park and it is relaxing and fun for the kids. Also, in McKinley Park they have hills, so in winter if there is snow you can sled. My father and I tried to go sledding but it didn't work that much. The snow wasn't hard and it wasn't deep.

In the summer, you can go to McKinley Park's pools. My whole family went to the pool there and we had fun. I was old enough to go to the adult pool instead of the preschool pool that has really low waters. The big pool is actually not that big but it has a diving board. My dad jumped off of the diving board and I enjoyed watching him.   —*Krystal Peña, grade 3*

illustration by Maryann Alejandre, grade 2

» TRANSLATION ON PAGE 235

HELADO *y* PALETAS *con* TUS AMIGOS

MCKINLEY PARK ES un lugar muy fabuloso para tener una grande fiesta y jugar con amigos. Tiene una alberca hay grande y otro para niños pequeños y te puedes divirtir mucho. Las albercas están afuera. Durante el invierno están cerradas. Durante el verano puedes comer helado y paletas con tus amigos. Alguien está vendiendo la comida en un cartero. Puedes jugar con los colimpios y hay unas grandes y otros más chicos. Hay muchas resbaladillas. Hay un grande lago y cerca puedes ir a jugar béisbol. Mi prima y yo a veces jugamos béisbol. Mi amiga, Gaby, tenía una fiesta allí para su cumpleaños. Nosotros jugamos tag y hide y seek afuera en el parque. Después había magíca y hasta hicieron muchísimos chistes. Luego nos dieron un pastel de chocolate delicioso. Encima del pastel tenía muchos dibujos de muñecos. Si está buscando un lugar para una fiesta debe ir a McKinley Park. —*Susana Zavala, grade 3*

A LOT *of* LIFE *in* THIS PARK

THE BEST PLACE to go to in my neighborhood is Peterson Park. It is right across the street from my house, which gives me a really good view of the park. Peterson Park is great because there is always some kind of event coming around. There are so many fun activities to do, such as visit the Nature Center. At the Nature Center you can learn about different animals and see how the animals live. After that, the people who work there give you a tour around the woods and you can see a lot of deer and birds, turtles, and a little pond with tiny fishys.

There are two playgrounds with monkey bars, a slide, and swings. There are also sandboxes. The playgrounds are a good size and are very fun. There are a lot of things for a kid to do. Peterson Park has a basketball court, tennis court, soccer fields, and a baseball diamond. When it gets warmer outside the soccer and baseball starts. There is a soccer game on Saturday and Sunday. Sometimes there are soccer festivals and it isn't just for the kids who play soccer; it's also for the kids who just want to have fun. The festival has food, raffles, rock climbing, and a lot more to do. There are always activities for friends and family to come and hang out. The fun never ends until 3:30. Peterson Park also has a movie night for families and friends. There's always a time when it's wet outside, but that doesn't stop the people from going, mostly because it's

FREE! They play the movies on a big screen with a projector in front.

There are lots of things to listen to at the park. When people have parties, you can hear them talking, hear the music, and smell barbecuing. I always hear the boys playing basketball and hear the balls bouncing. Sometimes you will hear people cheering for their kids. You can even hear the animals in the forest, but don't worry, there's a fence so the animals don't get through. And even if they do, they will never hurt you. Trust me, I've seen a lot of deer around the park!

I go to Peterson Park a lot with my dog, my dad, and my brother. We used to let her off the leash to run, but she runs really fast. We take her on the slide with us. If you want to have fun and keep your day going, you should go to Peterson Park. There's a lot of life in this park.   —*Cari E. Matos, grade 6*

NOT *as* PLAIN *as* OTHER PARKS

A GREAT PLACE to go is Ping Tom Park in Chinatown. To get to Chinatown you have to find a part of town that is not much like the other parts of town, and is a part of town that has a lot of Chinese people. When I went to Ping Tom Park with my cousins and their dad we all tried to catch bunnies. The park is near a lot of restaurants, and I think the bunnies are there to get food. The bunnies hopped so fast we were tired! My cousin's face was all red.

Ping Tom Park also has a trail that is very long with lots of flowers. It is a quiet place. We were always stopping at the water fountain because it was such a long walk. When we were on the trail there was a bench and we all sat on it. The park also has a lake to go fishing. I saw a man and his son and they caught a big fish.

Ping Tom Park is a lot of fun and I like going to it. It is not as plain as other parks I go to.   —*Julianna Villarreal, grade 3*

149

PARKS

THINGS *to* DO BOTH DAY *and* NIGHT

PULASKI PARK HAS many things to offer in both the day and the night. In the day, you can swim by yourself in the small pool, or you could go swimming in the big rectangular pool with your counselor. There is a shallow end but the counselors don't want you to run and jump in it because you could bust your head open.

At night they have parties in Pulaski Park and at the end of the day they show movies that have a lot of action in them. The park people give out free food like hot dogs, hamburgers, and soda. You should eat ketchup and cheese on the hamburger they give you. And on your hot dog you should have ketchup, mustard, and a little pickle.

One thing that is sad about Pulaski Park is that in November the swing set was torn down. There is nothing where it used to be. We miss the swing set but like the monkey bars. Sometimes you can climb so much that you get blisters and splinters all over your hands.   —*Christopher Diaz de Leon, Zachary Joiner, Ariteja Miller, and Maria Murillo, grade 2*

GREAT POOLS *to* REFRESH YOURSELF

RIIS PARK IS a great park. You've got to go there. It's by Narragansett Avenue. You can go to the pools and refresh yourself and they also have a lot of festivals. Once, I went to a carnival there with my mom, sister, and my brothers. There were lights of all colors and many fun games and rides. My favorite ride was the roller coaster. The roller coaster was just moving up and down in a zig-zag that went really high and really low. We also went on the bumper cars and I was crashing into my brother in the mechanical cars. When we all got hungry, we ate nachos with cheese, hotdogs, and we drank pop until we felt like we couldn't eat or drink any more.

After eating, we still wanted to have some more fun so we went to the Ferris wheel, but that was a bad idea. We felt like throwing up, but we didn't. We couldn't stop feeling dizzy but decided to go to the dragon coaster since it was just going up and down. After all of that, we were tired, but we still went to the haunted house so we could be calm and feel the excitement of the fun day we had had on that hot Saturday. I will never forget our day out and can't wait to go again. —*Stephany Jimenez, grade 5*

At Washington Park, we would get the most beautiful skin by lying in the shiny sun.

—*Victoria Caruth, grade 4*

If you drown in Riis Park, the lifeguard will save you.

—*Hoguer Villada, grade 4*

GOOD *for* EVERYBODY *of* EVERY COLOR

WASHINGTON PARK IS for everybody of every color: blacks, whites, Indians, Puerto Ricans and everybody go to this park. The park is pretty. It has lots of beautiful flowers. Flowers everywhere are blooming at the park. We pick them sometimes and give them to our mamas.

One of my favorite parts of Washington Park is that you can go swimming. If I were to plan my perfect day, me and my friend would go to the girls locker room to put on our bathing suits while my Auntie went to the store to get chips and juice for us. Me and my friend would put our towels on the ground. We would meet new people. If we made a friend while we were all wet, we'd know our new friend liked us for what's on the inside, not just the out-side. Then, when my Auntie got back from the store, all three of us would go in the sliding pool. We would also run through the sprinklers. When we dried off and put our regular clothes on we would leave the pool.

You can spend the whole day at Washington Park. On my perfect day I would try and do everything that they have for you. I would try the monkey bars, the twisty slide and would go to the big area where people ride bikes. I would jump rope, too. You could also play hide and seek since the park has tall wide trees that you can hide behind. You could also hide under the slide.

153

PARKS

I love to read so on my perfect day I would take a book and sit under one of the big trees and just read and read.

—*Ashley Harris, grade 4*

FIND YOURSELF SOME PEACE *and* QUIET

WICKER PARK IS the best place to play. It is a great place to play because they have swings for big kids and babies. The slides there are a like a big roller coaster, especially if you are pretty small. They even have benches if you want to rest. They're really mostly for your parents to sit on. If you don't want to play there because you think it's for little kids, it's also a great place to hang out with your friends or with the cousins you miss. Wicker Park is a place you can just be if you want to find yourself some peace and quiet. Well, you can have peace and quiet when everyone is gone, of course.

The park has always been lucky to me. One day, I was sliding down the slide and I went so fast I fell off. A little girl said, "Hi, I'm Daisy." I got up and said, "Hey, want to get a soda?" She said, "Sure!" I knew we would be friends from that day and still we are the best of friends.

When we go to the park we usually wait until it gets dark and then we tell scary stories. My friends like to creep up behind me and scare me. Sometimes I like to show up late, sneak up behind them, and pop out and scare them. They get mad at me but I am just getting them back.   —*Nicole Manriquez, grade 5*

TAIL-SNIFFING MADNESS

WIGGLY FIELD, a dog park, is a place of tail-sniffing madness. It is also, of course, home of the Chicago Hounds. They are tail-wagging wieners and they're ready to take on the Bulldogs or any other Chicago team because they train on the park's obstacle course.

I go to Wiggly Field with my friends and their dogs, but can't go with my dogs. Bailey, my cute white American Eskimo, doesn't like other dogs that much, but he does like me and my family. He is very protective and doesn't like people he doesn't know. He is also a scaredy cat. He is a really fast runner. Beachness is also my dog. She is a pit bull and an awesome friend. She likes people and not dogs, and cuddles all the time. I love her so much because she is a cuddle monster.

Wiggly Field has so much to do. Dogs like it because they can go off their leashes without getting in trouble. Show dogs sometimes have obstacle courses. Other dogs talk to each other. And a lot of dogs run around really fast. One time I was playing with my friend's dog and another dog came and jumped from a boulder up to my head. His owner came and got him off. I was laughing. That is an example of how Wiggly Field is not just a place where dogs meet, but people meet there, too!   —*Olivia Vanoverbeke, grade 4*

6 | *neighborhoods*

THE MOST BALLIN' BLOCK

MY BLOCK IS BALLIN' because it's hot. The block is on 50th and Halsted. We have fun on this block. We have dance contests. The contests happen when it's hot. They happen outside, in front of our houses. Someone brings a radio and we play CDs. Two people dance against each other and everyone else judges. It keeps going until we get tired. Sometimes we go to the park. This is hangin'. The park is at Dewey School. We jump rope, play hide-n-seek, and swing.

I have lived here in a really big house for two years. I live with my brother, Jerry, mom, Delores, and my step-dad, John. We have Young's Candy Store on the block. I buy hot chips at Young's Candy Store. I go there everyday after school. Down the street is a mall. Chernin's Shoe Store is a store I go to a lot.

When you come to my block, you see houses, big apartment buildings, and a church. When I go to school, I catch the bus by myself. When I go any place else, I travel in a car with my mom, brother, and sometimes my step-dad.

I love my block because it's fun. New kids who move to the block mean new friends. One of my friends just moved: her name is Shay-Shay. One of my best friends is about to move. Her nickname is Vanilla. I will miss her and I know she will miss me, but we will still see each other.

That's why my block is ballin'. —*Latashia Cardine, grade 6*

159

NEIGHBORHOODS

In Chicago, you will find a lot of entertainment and people telling jokes. Trust me, you will laugh so hard you will start crying.

—*Stefany Rebollar, grade 4*

DANCE-OFFS *with* FOOTWORK

ON MY BLOCK, 69th and Wabash, we have street parties. In July, we block off the streets about two times and set up games, jumping jacks, and food. We have dance-offs with footwork and do the "walk-it-out," the "pop," and the "bomb." Jump rope contests are also popular.

The food at our street parties is delicious. There's spaghetti, whole fried and grilled fish, grilled chicken, pork chops, hot links, and special barbecue sauce. My favorites are the spaghetti and chicken. For dessert, I like ice cream, with either Snickers or cookies. You can also get cotton candy. Sometimes, when we're not looking, the people on the streets sneak in through the backyard and steal some of the food!

At the block party, we also play street basketball and football. I play basketball because I don't know how to play football. The winners get to split a prize of some money. My strongest memory of our block parties was when it rained last summer. It rained really hard and everybody started running, grabbing everything along the way. Some people still went out with umbrellas and played in the puddles. Even though it rained, it was still fun. —*Tierra Washington, grade 6*

HELP *with* SCHOOLWORK, HELP *with* SPYING

826CHI IS A great place to go when you need help with your homework. I am very famous there because of the funny things that I do. At 826CHI, they have nice tutors, good games, and interesting workshops. They also have a store called The Boring Store that sells spy stuff, like one thing that can x-ray your pockets. 826CHI is right in my neighborhood, Wicker Park.

One weekend at 826CHI, I went to a workshop that was led by a tutor named Carrie. The workshop was about knitting and I got to make a scarf and write a letter to the person I was making it for. I am going to give the scarf to my mom and give her the letter that says she is the best mom in the world.   —*Yemisi Ososami, grade 4*

illustration by Jaime Palatox, grade 4

WINNING *the* JOB *of* PRESIDENT

BARACK OBAMA MEANS a lot to Chicago and to my neighborhood. I live on the West Side and he does a lot of things for our community. He's always there for us. Obama is hoping to become the next candidate for president. He is a great business worker. He is always busy doing things. He is a great leader for parents and kids because he inspires lots of people. My grandma says Barack Obama made her believe that she can follow her dreams.

Barack Obama is a tall man with light brown skin. He is married and he has one or two kids, I think. I want him to win the job of president. Barack Obama was in Springfield, Illinois, last week when he was giving his big speech about running for president. I was watching it on TV with my mom, my grandma, and my sister. My mom and my grandma said they're going to vote for him. A lot of people in my neighborhood want him to be president.

Barack Obama has inspired so many people today and a lot of people are hoping he'll win because he will be the first African-American president. I think that he is going to make this world a better place to live in. He'll make communities better and I really think that all of Chicago would be proud if he became president because he is from our city! —*Tasia Drake, grade 5*

MAKE ROBBERS RUN

MY FAVORITE PLACE in my neighborhood is Chang's Tae-Kwan-Do. It is located a couple of blocks from my school, West Belden. At Chang's, you learn how to defend yourself. If someone tries to rob you they show you how to make them run. You are taught ways of fighting and tactics that are used for self-defense. Tae-Kwon-Do is not to be used on people who are not a threat, because you might hurt them badly. At Chang's, you make friends really fast. I met Kevin, Bryant, Michael, and a couple of Josés.

One day, Kevin's mom took Kevin, his brothers, my brother, and me to Tae-Kwan-Do. She was the one who always took us. The master's name is Pedro, but his students call him "Simini." Simini is his master name that only his students call him. He is strict, but a good teacher. I stopped going when I was an orange belt. I had already received my white and yellow belts.

We had to flip over people and...you'll know the rest if you go. I recommend Tae-Kwon-Do because it taught me how to jump over four people at once, which is something I never thought I could do.   —*Fernando Ramirez Gaytan, grade 5*

KIND *and* TRUTHFUL NEIGHBORS

MY FORMER NEIGHBORHOOD is a great place to visit because of the people. The West 72nd place area looks like a small little town. It has two train stations nearby. There are lots of trees and wonderful singing birds. I lived there with my family for eight or nine good years before we moved. We lived with my grandparents, who still live there.

In the house, on the first floor there are three bedrooms and one bathroom. Down in the basement, there are two bedrooms and one bathroom. I lived in the basement with my mom and my sister and my grandparents lived on the first floor. The people who live in my neighborhood are very kind and truthful.

Once my neighbors invited me to their home to eat dinner. They were also my friends. There are three kids in the family and one is my age. The other two are younger. We had tacos with beans, lettuce, tomato, and chicken. When I was done with my homework, I went to play outside. Once I got outside, I played hide-and-seek, Johnny Come Across and tag. The friends from the neighborhood I played with have different cultures. Two of them are Mexican. The others are African, Puerto Rican, and Columbian. All the people are exciting and sometimes quiet. I like to go back when I visit my grandparents.   —*Diana Sanchez, grade 6*

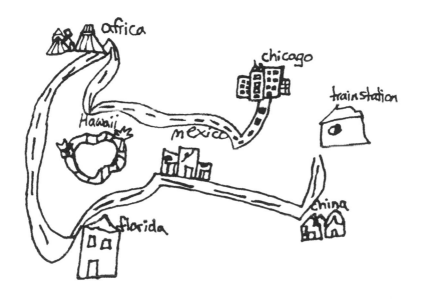

illustration by Ivette Rucobo, grade 4

SPICES LIKE CURRY

THE BEST PLACE to visit by my house is Devon Avenue. Devon is a street with Indian and Pakistani stores and restaurants. You can get to Devon by car, taxi, or bus because Devon has lots of bus stops.

One of my favorite restaurants is Tahoora. It smells like barbeque chicken and picoras cooking and you can hear waiters shouting out orders. Tahoora has the best kulfis. A kulfi is an ice cream blob on a stick. There are three flavors: mango, pistachio, and original. I like the mango flavor. The pistachio has nuts and I don't like nuts and the original flavor has no taste to me.

Sometimes a man walks around a store or block with a stick of different colored cotton candy. Once I was in the meat store with my dad and he gave me a dollar to go and get a blue cotton candy.

The smells on Devon are different than in another part of Chicago. You can smell spices like curry mixing with sweets like ice cream. It may sound bad but when you taste it, it's good!

My favorite shopping store is Sahil. It has two floors and it is very fancy. Sahil sells clothes, shoes, and lots of jewelry. I usually go there to buy jewelry or clothes. It's not very expensive, depending on what you buy or want. My mom took us to Devon to buy some groceries and we walked past Sahil. In the window, I saw a blue necklace with pink diamond–like stones. I felt like it was supposed to be mine. I begged my mom for it, but she said we had to hurry since we were having guests for dinner. I don't think my mom meant it when she said we'd buy it another time, but I still feel like I should have it. Maybe some day.

When I'm at Devon, I feel excited and alive because all of the great things to do there. *—Urooj Mahmood, grade 6*

YOUR SPRING CLEANING FIX

FLEETWOOD ROLLER RINK is the most fun place in Chicago. It is the best place in Chicago for many reasons. Most people get attracted to it because of the arcade, but I got attracted to it because of the roller skating. The roller rink is very wide and the skates are very cheap to rent. The DJs there play good modern music. They play Akon CDs, and Beyoncé, and so much more. Fleetwood Roller Rink is often is often very crowded, and that's good because that must mean it's really fun.

One reason Fleetwood is really good for me is because if you need help the staff members help you and teach you if you want to learn how to roller skate. They've helped me lots of times. I especially like Fleetwood's all-girls' skating time because all of the boys are in the arcade then and don't laugh at you when you fall.

When you leave Fleetwood Roller Rink you feel so energetic. One day me and my mom went and she got so full of energy that as soon as she got home she cleaned the house for two days straight. My dad said, "We should take her again some time."

—*Melanie de la Cruz, grade 5*

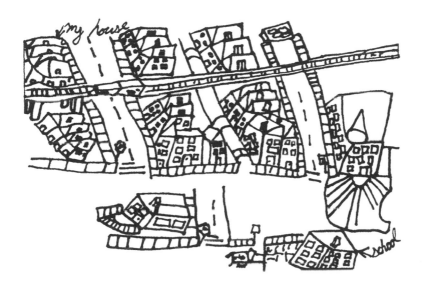

my house

school

illustration by Victor Zarah, grade 6

FROM HEAD SPINS *to the* CRYPT WALK

THE BEST THING to do in Chicago is to do a block party! Last year, my next-door neighbor threw a party for the neighborhood for about 150 people. My friends came and brought a stereo and I would break-dance. Some of the break-dancing moves I do are the worm, head spins and the crypt walk. When I got tired, me and my friends ate some hot dogs and cheeseburgers (because that is the best food to eat at a block party). After that, I went to my friend's back yard to swim in the pool. When we got out we ate some candy. Skittles, M&M's, and Snickers are my favorite and they were all at the block party. At the very end, we went onto the trampoline at 9 p.m. It was finished then and that was all we were going to do.   —*Luis Valenciano, grade 4*

HARDWORKING, ATHLETIC, *and* LOUD

WHEN I THINK ABOUT the important people in my neighborhood, I think the most important are the firefighters. They are safeguarding, helpful and nice. The firefighters work very hard; their jobs are challenging; and all of the firefighters are athletic.

The Lincoln Park firefighters came to my school once to make sure we would be safe if the school caught on fire. I was sitting in Spanish class when the fire alarm went off. We all jumped up and got in line. The firefighters were at the end of one hallway. They were smiling at us, so we knew it was not a real fire. At the end of the fire drill the firefighters beeped the horn and everyone jumped—even the teachers!

A reason I am such a fan of the firefighters is that once I saw on TV that a little girl's family's restaurant was burning because they accidentally left the stove on. When the firefighters came it still burned down, but they at least tried their best to take down the fire, which shows how dedicated they are to their jobs!

—*Leslie Canet, grade 5*

A BIG BACKYARD *and a* GREAT VIEW

THE BEST THING about Marquette is that I live in a great apartment building. It has a big backyard, so I can play football. I love football. I also live close to my Auntie. I like to see her a lot. I have been living in Marquette for five years, and that's a long time.

The other thing I like about Marquette is that I live very, very close to my school and, because of that, I am not late a lot. I'm so close to school that I can look over the balcony and see my friends at the park. I can see my teacher through the classroom window, too.

Every weekday, I walk home with my sister after school. My neighborhood is a very nice neighborhood because I have lots of friends. Sometimes when I go outside, it's noisy because of the cars. It smells because of the dogs and other animals. I still like the neighborhood though. I guess every neighborhood has some noise and some smelly animals!

My favorite thing about where I live is that I live next to a lot of stores on 71st street. The Harold's Chicken has a great mild sauce, and at McDonald's I order either a chicken sandwich or a double cheeseburger. I also go to a store called Big Dollar. They have toys, radios, and games. There is a movie theatre close by, too. I go to the show with my mom, sometimes my dad, and once in a while I get to take a friend. I like action adventure movies the best.

—*Daryl Gatewood, grade 6*

illustration by Alma Rosa Banda Leon, grade 2

TEACHING MATH *to* KIDS

THE MOST IMPORTANT Chicago person to me is my teacher Ms. Klink. Ms. Klink teaches fifth grade at Alcott School in Lincoln Park. She helps a lot of the kids in the neighborhood. I can describe her like this: she has brown hair and she is tall. The next thing is that she is skinny, helpful, caring, and loving to me. Ms. Klink is also a smart person in the neighborhood. She is the best teacher I've had! She teaches math to kids.

Some kids say Ms. Klink is a very hard worker and that she helps a lot of people like me. She is a hard worker because before she teaches something in math, she thinks about what she is going to say. And if she messes up, she rethinks it over again. I say that she has a great attitude in school, because when the sixth grade gets crazy she holds her yelling in and just goes and sits at her desk without getting mad.

One day Ms. Klink was walking to the overhead with some papers and she tripped over a chair that was pulled out. Everyone started laughing and she did too. She didn't take it as seriously as I thought she would. This tells me she is funny.

Ms. Klink is the most important person to me in Chicago. She is the best teacher I have in Chicago! Ms. Klink is also a very good teacher because she doesn't get a temper like some other teachers. She has us write lines instead. She also helps us with things that we

don't get right away. If I had to pick the best teacher in Chicago, it would be Ms. Klink. I love having her as my teacher.
—*Brittany Mills, grade 5*

A GREAT FIVE YEARS

MARQUETTE IS THE best neighborhood around the city of Chicago because we have lots of kids around and we all play football at the park or in the street. I get around my neighborhood by walking or driving in my Dad's car to places where we eat. We like to go to BaBa's where they have good food and drinks, nachos, hotdogs, milkshakes, and pop. My mom and I shop at Ford City Mall for clothes, shoes, and things that we need.

I live in a house here with my mom and dad and my two brothers. We've been living here for five years and it's been a great five years. We've had lots of parties there and lots of family has visited.

One of the things I would change in my neighborhood is the school park. I would change it to a good-looking school park and add some grass to the ground. A basketball rim would also be nice. And a football field. The second thing I would change is the bad kids in the neighborhood because they are disrespectful to adults and the kids and the neighborhood. Sometimes they throw trash on the ground and they say "shut up" to older people. That part is not good but the rest of the things about my neighborhood are. Marquette is a good block to live on.   —*Jamell Lincoln, grade 6*

SWORDS THAT FIGHT EACH OTHER

THE NOBLE HORSE THEATRE is a historical place in Chicago. The arena is covered with dirt. There are many rows with tables for the audience to enjoy. On weekends people are able to have a nice meal while watching the show.

When the horse show starts, it is pitch black. Then a light appears in the darkness and two men on horses start chasing each other. There is silence and no talking. They start fighting with swords, loud banging, and then more clattering swords. As they go away, their swords still fight each other. When I was there, one of the men came in and started doing tricks. He stood on the horse while the horse was going around a red circle.

The rest of the show has different performances in it. At the end of the shows, you can enjoy a horse ride, you can pet the horses, and for little ones you can go on a hayride. I would highly recommend this show for families. —*Itzel Castillo, grade 5*

THE DOGGIEST BLOCK

THE BEST THING about my neighborhood around North Central Park is that it has the doggiest block in Chicago. There is a different dog in each of my neighbor's homes. One thing I really like about the neighborhood's dogs is that none of them bite or bark at you. The neighborhood dogs are always happy to see someone and they always want to play. When you pass them on the street, they wag their tails and stick out their tongues. Trust me, if you come to my neighborhood, you will never get bored from looking at all the dogs.

My closest neighbor has a golden retriever. It is a year old. It is tall and fun to play with. His name is Max. You can usually find Max in his backyard playing fetch with his owner.

The house on the left of my closest neighbor has a small poodle. He is small and full of energy. That poodle is eight months old. His name is Burney and he is my favorite dog in the neighborhood because he can stand on his back legs on his own. But Burney will only do that trick if you promise him a treat.

My other neighbor has an American bulldog. The dog is three years old and his name is Grumpy. I don't know why his name is Grumpy because he is always playful and cheerful. I play tug of war with him. Grumpy always wins because he is so big and strong.   —*Kimberly Valdez, grade 5*

EVERY YARD GROWS FLOWERS

MY BLOCK'S NAME is Seeley and it's between Damen and Hoyne. My block is very special to me for many reasons. All my neighbors are nice and friendly. They greet people on the street. Every front lawn is nice, neat, and clean. Most every yard grows flowers. There are flowers in my yard, too. One of the best things is there are five stores across the street and they all sell ice cream! They sell both scoops of ice cream and bars. My favorite flavor is vanilla. When it's cold I get ice cream twice a week. When it's hot—everyday! I go with my big sister and she only eats vanilla, too.

The most important reason I like my block is because I feel safe there. I feel very calm because there is no one to harm me. There are no fights on my block. There are rules that everyone must follow, rules like no littering, no loud music, and no parking unless you live on the block. If you don't follow the rules, the president or vice president of the block can report you to the police.

My block also has a Fourth of July party. At the party there are contests for ring toss and basketball. They have jumping jacks and food like juice, candy, and chips. Everybody on the whole block comes to this party! That's why my block is so special. If you're looking to move to the best block in Chicago, come to the block Seeley! —*Jakira Black, grade 6*

DRIBBLING THROUGH OTHER PLAYERS' LEGS

I LOVE MICHIGAN AVENUE because there are lots of kids to play with. I play baseball with my friends Daryl, Lil Paris, Larry, and Terrell. Our team is called the Hot Shooters. We play against other teams almost every day. We win a lot. Our team's special move is dribbling through the other team's players' legs.

I have lived on Michigan Avenue for three years. I like my house so much that I never want to move. I have my own bedroom and a big backyard where I play football. My whole family likes to clean the house so that it looks nice and we won't have critters.

The house also has an alarm system, which is good because the neighborhood can be dangerous. I want to stop the shooting and killing. Sometimes, especially when it's hot outside, some people don't know how to act. There is shooting between the gangs, but I feel safe when I am inside my house.   —*Rashad Mitchell, grade 6*

7 | sports

SIX-FOOT TALL SMELLY SWEATY MEN

HAVE YOU EVER heard of the wonderful Chicago Bulls? Six-foot tall, smelly, sweaty men play on this team. The Bulls play basketball and their symbol is a bull. If you want to support them, you can wear their colors, red and black. I don't usually wear red and black together but I'll wear them at a Bulls game because I'm a fan.

The stadium is at the United Center. It has shiny wood floors. The crowd is always roaring, yelling "Boo!" or "Let's go! The smells at the stadium are both good and bad—food, drinks, and sweat.

I remember one time when Michael Jordan made a slam-dunk. The crowd cheered and I jumped up and down. Michael Jordan is very tall, almost as tall as the Sears Tower. This makes it easier for him to reach the hoop. He always sticks his tongue out when he makes a slam-dunk, which is funny and makes me laugh.

If you're ever in Chicago, drop by the United Center to see a Chicago Bulls game. Even though Michael Jordan isn't there anymore, you'll still have a great time and will go home with a hoarse voice from cheering. Hopefully they'll win the championships soon, and maybe you'll be in the audience cheering them on!

—*Hannah Berman, grade 5*

BOOING *and* MAKING MAD FACES

A GOOD PLACE to go in Chicago is the United Center. The United Center is special because the Bulls play there. At The United Center there is a line of rectangular banners hanging from the ceiling with all of the Bulls' championships written on them. Around the stadium, there are lots of TVs hanging down from poles on the ceiling. These TVs show commercials and games during the basketball game. They show basket-shooting races and rolling-across-the-floor races with different people. When you go to The United Center, you should always bring stuff with you like jerseys, money, and autograph paper, because you never know if you will see a Bulls player.

At the United Center, the players play so far beneath you that it seems like they are underground. If you have seats by the players it is sometimes cold, but the seats higher up are really warm. The time I went, I saw the Bulls play the 76ers. I was with my cousin. Every time the 76ers made a point, the crowd would boo and make mad faces. Every time the Bulls made a point the crowd would be happy and yell a lot. The Bulls won the game, and we got free burgers since they won. You should go to the United Center. You never know when you might get a free burger!

—*Ezekiel Alberty, grade 5*

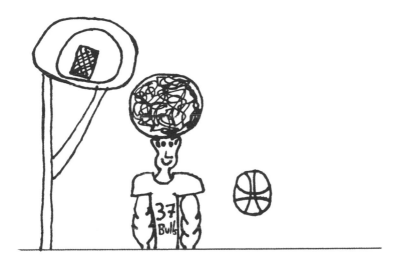

illustration by Janice Torres, grade 3

AN ALL-BOYS TEAM

COME TO CHICAGO and see the White Sox! The White Sox are an all-boys team. They are not all the same age; they are different. They are the South Side team, and the Cubs are the North Side team. The Sox have a logo that is a couple of S's with some lines in them. White and black are the colors of the White Sox's team.

The White Sox have a stadium that is huge! The name of the stadium is U.S. Cellular. The field is a combination of grass, dirt, and sand. Because the stadium is new it is clean, even shiny. Their stadium is the best in the whole city. (That's Chicago if you forgot!)

I went to the stadium a few years ago with my summer camp. The Cubs played the Sox. There were two or three home runs and after each one there were fireworks. My brother, sister and I got some nachos and some Sprites. We sat very high up, in one of the higher rows. It was really hot out and it made me tired, but it was very exciting, especially during the fireworks.

Chicago is really enthusiastic when one of their teams win. Two years ago, the White Sox won the World Series! I remember when we were at home watching TV. My cousins and my aunt and uncle came over to watch. We ate salsa and chips the whole time. And then it happened. Bam! They won! They won all of the games in a row!   —*Sarah Quander, grade 5*

BALLOONS WERE EVERYWHERE

IN 2005, I was getting ready so I could go to U.S. Cellular Stadium. My dad and family were dressed like the White Sox because my family likes the White Sox. I was so happy because it took the White Sox seven games to get into the World Series.

The U.S. Cellular Field stadium was crowded with a lot of people waiting to get inside. After forty minutes we went inside. It was really big and had a store where I bought a foam finger. Then I had a seat on a big bench while I waited for the game to start. I drank a Coke. The White Sox then began to play the game versus the Houston Astros. There was a big screen TV where I could watch the replays and I saw a banner flying around the stadium that said "U.S. Cellular."

After a lot of time, the game was almost over and the Sox were winning. Then the game finished and the White Sox had won the World Series. The Sox are my favorite team and I would love them even though they hadn't won, but I'm glad they did! After the game, one of the players signed a ball for me. In the stadium, there were balloons everywhere.   *Maico Uzhca, grade 5*

The Cubs' whole team's players are boy players. No women—boooo!

—*Nia Lee, grade 5*

PLAYING ON CHANNEL 60 *or* 64

THE BEST TEAM in Chicago is the Chicago Fire. The Chicago Fire got its name because of an accident that happened in Chicago a long time ago. A fire started and went fast through the city because almost everything was made of wood then. The team has a new stadium that was built in 2005. They didn't have a stadium before that. The Chicago Fire won the first game they played in that stadium. I haven't been there but my cousin told me it was big, like Soldier Field. Maybe one day I'll go to see the Chicago Fire at the stadium with my brother, but you don't have to go to the stadium to see them play. You can watch a game on TV. You can see them playing on channel 60 or 64 on cable.

The Chicago Fire has the best goalie, the best defense, and they have Eddie Johnson on their team. He is a player on the U.S.A. soccer team. Their defense is strong because they are focused on the game. —*Juan Suarez, grade 5*

IT STARTED *with a* LEGEND

WHY SHOULD YOU come to Chicago? Well, to see the Chicago Fire, of course! They're a soccer team, the one and only. The Chicago Fire started with a legend. On the 126th anniversary of the Great Chicago Fire it was decided that the new Major League Soccer team belonging to Chicago would be called the Chicago Fire. There are only boys on the team: unfortunately, no girls are allowed! I think it would be better if there were boys and girls on the team. I play soccer and I'd like to play for the Chicago Fire.

The colors of the Chicago Fire are red and white. And what is their mascot, you ask? A Dalmatian! The Dalmatian wears a firefighter's helmet and a Chicago Fire jersey. By the way, in case you were wondering, the members of the team range from 16 to thirty-two years of age.

The Chicago Fire has a clean, nice, new stadium. It is out in the suburbs. It has a paved track that is black. The field is grassy and is well taken care of. The stadium itself has many entrances. Unlike some stadiums, the bleachers are permanent.

When I went to a game myself, I saw the Chicago Fire win a game against the New England Revolution. Since it was the first game of the season, the team let fans walk their dogs around the track. I brought my dog Luna. During the game, yellow cards—actually seven yellow cards—were given out in total. Yellow cards are violations given out when one player of a team pushes down another player on the opposite team. During the game, three yellow cards were given to New England and four to the Chicago Fire. That game was a blast! The fans got so into it that it was almost like being part of the game.   —*Samantha Kosloske, grade 5*

GOING *with* MY FAMILY'S DECISION

CHICAGO IS THE best place for sports. Most of all, it is the best because of the Cubs. Right now they're not playing that well, but I still like them. The reason I like them is that my family was encouraging me to vote for the Cubs. My father collected sports cards and kept them in an album. He collected a lot of the Cubs. Also, I remember my mom kept pointing at the Cubs on TV and saying, "That's our team! They rule!" so I went with their decision. Another reason why I like the Cubs is that I went to a Cubs game and it was as big as three baseball fields there. Or, I thought it was. I was younger and it looked like three million people could fit into the seats. It was the coolest day of my life.   —*Crystal Reyes, grade 5*

THE TEAM *with* SERIOUS FACES

THE BLACKHAWKS ARE a tough team. They play hockey and are famous. There are only guys on the team. The guys are all twenty years old. They are harsh and focused.

I used to play hockey like the Blackhawks when I was young. The team I played on was called the Poison Green Frogs. There were ten girls on the team. We chose the name Poison Green Frogs over Pink Elephants because it sounded tougher. My dad came to every Poison Green Frogs game.

While I was playing hockey, my dad took me to a Blackhawks game so I could see if I could learn from the best players. I noticed that the Blackhawks had serious faces. They didn't look to the crowd to see their friends. They focused on the game. I learned to not look for my parents in the crowd during the game but just to look at the other team. I learned from the Blackhawks to put my head in the game.

If the Blackhawks weren't so serious, and if they would've looked into the crowd, what they would've seen was that my dad was sleeping! He fell asleep during the Blackhawks' game! My Poison Frogs games must have been more exciting for my dad, since he never fell asleep during those.   *Ramsha Khawar, grade 5*

VERY SMELLY PEOPLE WITHOUT DEODORANT

MY SO-SO FAVORITE team is the Cubs. They play at Wrigley Field. It is a very large place inside and out. At the game, there were very, very smelly people in the hot, hot sun without deodorant. They smell like beer. All the men had about seven cups of beer. They had hamburgers, beer, hot dogs, candy, Gatorade, soda, more beer, water, and more beer. My mom had popcorn. My teachers had soda. My mom really likes Sammy Sosa as a player and when he hit a home run she screamed and screamed again.

—*Zach Moore, grade 5*

WATCHING SOMEONE ELSE CATCH *the* BALL

THE BEST PLACE in my neighborhood is Wrigley Field, home of the Chicago Cubs. I think Wrigley Field is the best because when you deposit your ticket at the front desk the mascot is giving away coloring books and other activities for little kids to do during the game. I didn't use mine: I gave it to my little sister since I would rather watch the game.

By the personal boxes at Wrigley Field there are beautiful flowers to look at. When you're hungry you can personalize your own pretzel with candy, cinnamon, chocolate chips, or whatever you please. We usually go to Wrigley Field on my dad's birthday. My first game was the day after my dad's birthday. It was really rainy, and the Cubs won. After the game, they set up a big mat, like a Slip 'N Slide, and the players would run and slide on the mat. Me and my parents stayed and watched. My dad was laughing and we wished that we had a camera. Then, when we were leaving we saw a wedding going on, and the bride and groom were getting their picture taken in front by the sign that says "Wrigley Field".

When the Cubs are playing at Wrigley Field there is always a blimp with "Go Cubs." When you go by Wrigley Field on nights when the Cubs won, there are fireworks! The best part of Wrigley Field is if it's your birthday and you tell the workers they will either sing to you or put it on the billboard. Also, when you watch a game at Wrigley Field you can catch the ball. When I watch a game at home, I just watch someone else catch the ball and then wish it was me.   *—Olyvia Puente, grade 5*

A MUSEUM *on the* BOTTOM *and* ALL SHINY *on* TOP

MY FAVORITE FOOTBALL team ever is the Chicago Bears. The last time the Bears won the Super Bowl was in 1985 when their coach was Mike Ditka. Now the Bears have excellent defense and an excellent linebacker named Brian Urlacher. Brian Urlacher is a good linebacker because he is huge and he is very strong. The Bears also have a talented punt returner named Devin Hester. He is very fast and good at dodging other players.

The Bears' stadium is called Soldier Field. They play in it when it is mostly cold and windy. The stadium is now bigger than it was before. I've never seen a Bears game there, but I was inside Soldier Field once when I was very little. I don't remember why I was there, but I remember how it looked like a museum on the bottom and was all shiny on the top.

One of my favorite times watching the Bears is when they played against the Saints. I watched the game at my house with my dad and his friends. We had tons of pizza and every time the Bears scored a touchdown, everybody got up and yelled. The Bears were in the lead and they were forced to make a field goal. Robbie Gould kicked the football and the ball traveled to the side. Then he made the field goal and the crowd went wild and the Bears defeated the Saints. My dad picked me up and shook me and all his friends were screaming. —*Tristan Kagan, grade 5*

FEEL THEIR SWEAT DRIPPING OFF *of* THEM

EVEN THOUGH THE Bears lost the Super Bowl they are still number one. Some of the best players on their team are Thomas Jones, Brain Urlacher, Tank Johnson, Robbie Gould, Mushin Muhamed and Devin Hester. They are hard workers because if they weren't, they wouldn't have made it to the Super Bowl. All along the way I always thought that the Bears were going to win the Super Bowl because of the way that Hester ran that touchdown. The Bears have a great coach. His name is Lovie Smith. The bears also have a great history because of Papa Bear Halas. Do you know that Papa Bear Halas was the first one to invent the interception and also the field goal?

The Bears play in a stadium that is so humongous that it is the size of fifty basketball courts. It is called Soldier Field and is also a landmark, at least in my mind. Soldier Field is so old that they had to rebuild it. When you go there, they always have great food, like hot dogs, pizza, and any kind of pop.

The Bears are so famous that some people who don't even know them cheer for them. I watch all the games, usually with my aunt, my uncle, or my two cousins. I hope that if I can't be there, you can be there watching the Bears for me, and that you are so close to them you can feel their sweat dripping off of them.

—*Betty Tyler, grade 5*

illustration by Esteban Licea, grade 4

GIVING *the* PLAYERS COURAGE

THE BEARS. Doesn't it make your tongue tingle? It sure makes mine do so. Why does it make my tongue tingle? Because the Bears are the best football team in the United States and the best player (to me) is Brian Urlacher. Brian Urlacher tackles the other team's players before they even get to the goal. And he tackles really hard. The Bears are a great team and they never forfeit a game.

The Bears have a lot of traditions that I don't think a lot of other teams have, and the Bears remember their traditions very much. One of them is that the Bears and their fans still remember their dead player, Walter Payton. I first saw the Bears on TV when I was seven or eight. I liked them because they kept on winning games. I will be a Bears fan until I die! Even if the Bears lose, fans like me will wear the team's jerseys to show that we are still fans. We cheer the players on and give them courage.   —*Curtia James, grade 5*

The Bulls' mascot is Benny the Bull. He used to work at Best Buy.

—Olivia Alden, grade 5

I COULDN'T BELIEVE MY EYES

THE BEST SPORTS team in Chicago is the Bears. The Bears always tried their best and this year I couldn't believe my eyes when I saw that they were going to the Super Bowl. Even when it rained a lot during some of the games, they still played hard. Also, the Bears work together as a team, which is nice.

The day that the Bears were in the Super Bowl was a special day. I was with my family. We were all together and ate tamales and popcorn. We drank juice and water. We had fun.

During the Super Bowl, I was so excited when the Bears made a touchdown in the very first play! I was proud that they made a touchdown before the other team. They still have to keep trying until they make it to win the final game, but I will keep supporting them in the good times and the bad times. —*Heidi Torres, grade 5*

8 | *events*

COOL THINGS THAT MARCH THROUGH CHINATOWN

THE CHINESE NEW YEAR parade is the most exciting thing I did in my life! The Chinese New Year parade is a very loud place. Lots of people come to watch and take pictures. There are bands, floats, drums, dragon dances, and other cool things that march through Chinatown. I played there with James Ward School even though my real school is Mark Sheridan. My mom works at James Ward School so I had to go with her. I played on a red, shiny drum that I wore on my waist.

At the parade, there were many floats. One had Ronald Mc-Donald on it. There were also marching bands. One of them had orange shirts, and another one had bagpipes. The one that had bagpipes wore green all over. There was also a part of the parade where three people were in a lion costume. One person was the head and two were the body. Someone marched with them playing a big flat drum on wheels. That drum was four times as big as the one I played.   —*Jeffrey Lyang, grade 3*

207

EVENTS

AN INSIDER'S LOOK *at* RACECARS

IF YOU COME to Chicago in February, be sure to go to the Auto Show located at McCormick Place. At the Auto Show, they will have cars that will come out in the same year the Auto Show is held, or the next year after that. If you wander around sometimes there will be a racecar that you can get in and take pictures.

When I was looking at the cars, I found one I really liked. I looked closer and found out it was called a Hummer. What I liked about it was that it was my favorite color, had a lot of cool stuff like a GPS, and there was a TV in it.

During the Auto Show, they have the prices before they show the public. They let you see the inside of the car and you can go inside cars they have on display, too. They sometimes auction the cars they are showing before they come out. One time I got into a racecar and afterwards found out that it was actually used in a race! —*Julian Martinez, grade 6*

illustration by Alejandro Chiquito, grade 5

GYMNASTICS *and* FLEXIBLE ACTS

"LOOK!" "WOW!" "WHAT IS THAT?" Those are phrases you've heard if you have gone to the St. Patrick's Day parade. When I went, I saw girls and boys of all ages in green, both in the crowd and in the parade. They were all wearing green and doing some sort of activity! I especially liked the people doing gymnastics and flexible acts. Also, if you have been there, you have been shoved by someone. That's why I stood on the cement blocks that border Millennium Park. From there I watched everything without being shoved or yelled at by someone screaming, "Move your head!" or "I can't see!" While I was there I noticed that they...dyed the river GREEN! I couldn't believe it myself for a while and it is still very surprising.

The St. Patrick's Day parade is a lot of fun. If you were there I would have handed you a four-leaf clover.   —*Odessa Cody, grade 5*

SEE *the* EARTHWORMS FIGHTING

SPRING IN CHICAGO is rainy and it smells like water. It also smells like dirt. During spring, the earthworms crawl out of the ground and you can put them in jars. Sometimes you can even see the earthworms fighting with each other.

Springtime is a time when there are buds on the trees and ladybugs and ants are looking for food. The birds sing songs and eat the bugs and the worms. The caterpillars come out and eat leaves. And crickets sing with their legs in the night. They also jump around like they're dancing.

In the spring, you can ride your bike in the park or skateboard down the sidewalk. You can climb in the trees and jump in puddles. You can also play soccer in the park during spring, but you have to be sure to bring four orange or red cones.

—*Irvin Arrellano, Ricardo Barron, David Monte DeOca, and Ekyra Singleton, grade 2*

illustration by Andrea Castillo, grade 6

A BIKE RIDE *and* SOME MACARONI

MY FAVORITE THING to do in the summer is to ride my bike at my granny's house. The summer is the best time to ride bikes because you can feel your hair being blown and can feel the air on your skin. My bike is pink and white with purple pedals and brakes. I keep my bike at my granny's because if I keep it at home, it will make the apartment dirty inside.

I like to visit my granny once a week. Her name is Liza. She is fifty-two years old but looks like she is forty. Some people who are fifty-two look much older than my granny. She wears tight clothes and gets her hair done, her nails done, and her feet done. Sometimes she lets me paint her toenails. My grandaddy's name is Larry and you can tell he likes my granny a lot because of how he looks at her.

Most of the time when I'm at my granny's house, I like to ride my bike by myself. When I do, I enjoy the quiet and usually am thinking about what my granny will cook for me when I get home. Sometimes my Auntie rides with me. I like it when we ride together most of the time because we get to talk about the people and things we're passing, but one bad thing about riding with my Auntie is that she is sometimes distracted. She is always on the phone and she doesn't watch where she is going.

There is only so long I can ride before my stomach starts

growling. Usually my granny knows and she cooks me some dinner while I'm gone. My granny usually cooks chitlins, candied yams, and greens for her and my aunt, and for me she cooks macaroni. After dinner I wash up and think about what I'll do the next day. When I leave my granny's house, sometimes I cry because I know I'm going to miss her. *—Johnesha Turner, grade 3*

214

THE WHOLE HOUSE *is* LIKE *an* ALARM

I AM A BIG fan of the school year and I work hard all year long. I consider myself a good student and get mostly A's and B's. (Every once in a while I get a C in math but that's because of the times tables and division.) One reason I'm such a good student because Ms. Shea is a good teacher. Ms. Shea gives me a lot of responsibility in the classroom. When I get home I don't stop or undress or anything and I start my homework right away. My mom helps me and she is really smart, especially in geography.

At the end of the school year, and on the first day of summer, I'm usually so tired from working so hard all year that I just want to go to sleep. At the beginning of the summer, I sleep for three days, and I do not eat any meals at all. At 1:00 p.m. on the third day of summer, I wake up and then I am ready for summer vacation. I have so much energy from so much sleeping and I feel like I have to get around! I turn up the music as high as it can go and the whole house is like an alarm. My mama makes me some food. My first summer meal is mashed potatoes and corn bread. We drink Pepsi, Diet Pepsi, Coke, Coca-Cola, and Root Beer.

One of my favorite memories from last summer is when my grandma visited. My grandma, my mom, brother, sister and I relaxed like we were in New York. It would have been perfect if my dad was there but he had to work. To celebrate our day, we went to the beach. At the beach we used my surfboard. I fell a lot. On the way to the beach we bought a whole bucket of daisies and took one of the daisies to the beach. I like the daisy because it brings happiness to my family. I love the smell of the daisy because it smells like Jessica London perfume. We also bought some orange juice on our way and some cups that were way too big. Every time we poured juice into the cups it looked like there was hardly any there since the cups were so huge! This day was special because my family spent a most beautiful time together.

—*Pauletta Kelley, grade 3*

IN *a* DREAM WORLD FIGHTING PILLOWS

SUMMER IS MY favorite season in Chicago because it is when there is the most to do. During the summer, I like to go to the zoo, play football, golf with my granddad and daddy, look at movies with my family, eat pizza at the show, play softball on the weekend, put game helmets on, ride bikes five miles a day on the weekend, watch people-owners feed the dolphins at the aquarium, swim in the hotel pool, and eat popcorn, hot dogs, macaroni, and spaghetti. When I go outside during the summer the clouds make me feel like I am in a dream world fighting pillows, and the grass makes feel like I am in Ireland with the leprechauns.   —*Joshua Esters, grade 3*

illustration by Michael Anderson, grade 4

JETS FLYING OVER YOUR HEAD

THE CHICAGO AIR and Water Show is the largest plane and boat show in the United States, and it's totally free. If you like loud noise and jets, you will like the air and water show. I go to the show every year with my family because I want to be a Navy Pilot. My favorite jets in the show are the six Blue Angels.

The Blue Angels and the other jets practice flying right over my house! I can see them in my back yard but the best place to see all the other planes and boats is from North Avenue Beach or Oak Street Beach. You can also watch the show from Diversey Harbor. I bring my fishing pole and I go fishing with my dad and my brothers. We watch tons of jets fly over our heads while we catch our fish. My mom always brings a blanket and some food for us, too. —*Kevin Mendel, grade 2*

VEGETARIANS THAT EAT HOT CHIPS

IN SUMMER IN Chicago we are very busy, mostly playing in Riis park. It is fun to swing on the swings, unless you're like Jacqueline and don't know how to swing yet. It is also fun to cook meats on the grill, unless you're Lorena. She is a vegetarian. She used to eat chicken but doesn't anymore. Now she just eats hot chips.

Summer is a good time to go away from Chicago too, on vacations. Some good places to go are Mexico, New York, South Carolina, and the pool in Ulises's aunt's big yard.　—*Lorena Alvarado, Ulises Maldonado, Sergio Perez, Jacqueline Tapia, and Jeremy Wilson, grade 2*

illustration by Collette Gordon, grade 2

IMPORTANT, FAMOUS BANDS, *and* CONTESTS

HAVE YOU EVER been to a festival in the summer? I've been to lots, but one of my favorites is the Folk and Roots Festival in Welles Park. The festival takes up almost the entire park, with a lot of stages, stalls, and tents. The main stage hosts important, famous bands, and contests. There is also a kids' tent, an arts and crafts tent—which always has a fun project or two for kids who get bored—and the staff tent, where my friends Maddy and Charlotte hang out when their parents are performing. There are port-a-potties with sinks outside that never work, and you can buy food and trinkets at stalls in the surrounding streets. I usually get pizza and sometimes lemonade from the stall with the long line. I play guitar and sing in La Estudiantina, a class from the Old Town School of Folk Music nearby. It performs in the kids' tent, usually on Saturday. The festival takes up a weekend and I go on both days. I love performing and listening to music at the Folk and Roots Festival, and you should go there when it comes around this year.   —*Sheila McIntosh, grade 5*

THAT DAY I FELT LIKE VANILLA

CHICAGO IS THE best city, but the coolest thing is the beach. The beach I love is called North Avenue Beach. It has a big boathouse in the sand. I went with my dad and he bought a surfboard at this boathouse. He tried to ride it but he kept falling. I tried it but I only stood on it for two minutes. Then my sister tried to ride and she did it. We were all impressed. She is three years older than me and is cool. I learn a lot from her.

Our new dog was with us, too. He was a little brown and black dog and his name was Cuzco. We played with him in the water. Me, my dog, and my sister were having a swimming contest. Our dog won! After that we bought some ice cream. That day I felt like vanilla. We got one for my dog and he swallowed it in a huge gulp. Then we went home. I think that was my best day ever. I love to spend time with my family at the beach.   *—Nikolas Gonzalez, grade 4*

THE MAIN DAY *for* SKELETONS

DURING DAY OF THE DEAD, we celebrate, have a party, and dress up as dead people. We wear ghost and skeleton masks and paint our faces like we're the dead. It's a great day to take pictures because it is the main day when there are so many skeletons around.

In school, we like to do creepy art projects. You can make a cut-out of a skeleton and then make him dance if you attach yarn to his arms and legs. Once we performed a skeleton puppet show for our parents and families. We all wore masks that we made ourselves out of paper. Some masks had bones, three eyes, and spiders. Everyone wanted to take pictures of us. We sang and danced on stage and were mad that we made a mistake. (We forgot to clap, but nobody noticed.) —*Yulisa Flores, Eduardo Mentado, Cynthia Ochoa, and Michael Roman, grade 2*

PEOPLE PRETENDING *to* SUFFER

THE HALLOWEEN FESTIVAL in Daley Plaza is the most intriguing place in Chicago. When you go there you'll see a haunted house, a stage, and some bleachers. At the Halloween Festival they have an incredible show called the Midnight Circus. It is during the day.

During the show, you'll see jugglers, tightrope walkers, acrobats, and dancers. It is hard to believe how much fire the actors eat! Once I went there and someone was eating fire while walking on a tight rope. Then someone else blew fire on the rope. The tightrope walker almost got burned! After that, one of the actors actually caught fire but, luckily, the other actors brought in a tub of water. The guy who was on fire tripped off of the tightrope and fell into the water. It looked like an accident but it was really part of the show.

Another thing that they have at the Halloween Festival is a lot of carved pumpkins. Some are plain and look like something you can do at home. Others are very interesting and it intrigues you how people could actually carve that way. One of the pumpkins I saw had ten eyes and the person who made it took the shavings and made them into horns. It also had three mouths, five noses, arms, and feet. I don't think I could ever make a pumpkin like that because the mouths looked very intricate and had good teeth, and the arms and feet looked real.

225

EVENTS

I've gone to the Halloween Festival most years but I've missed it twice. I usually go with my dad and my sister. They like it as much as I do. I think anyone who likes funny things, plays, and carved pumpkins should go there. But if you don't like to see people pretending to suffer, don't go.   —*Harold Carpenter, grade 3*

226

CHOKED BY YOUR OWN SCARF

ON THE FIRST DAY of winter we feel happy about playing in the snow all winter long. We also feel cold. During December, January, and February in Chicago it is a snowy time with no leaves on the trees. Chicago winters are like winters in the North Pole. It gets so windy that sometimes the branches fall down.

To survive the winter, you should eat warm foods like soup and drink hot chocolate. You must also put on warm clothes when you go outside or you'll be freezing! Brrrr! To stay warm, you need to wear a huge jacket, a warm hat to keep your ears warm, and a scarf. Sometimes the scarf chokes you, so don't put your scarf on too tight. *Santiago Aguilera, Christopher Alfaro, Jasmin Buhena, Sean Carrillo, and Natalia Morales, grade 2*

BECOME *a* CHAMPION

DO YOU WANT to have fun in the winter? Go ice skating. It is one of my favorite things to do. You might slip and fall, but just practice.

If you slip and fall you can bring a camera to share and laugh at good memories. Bring band-aids in case you scrape your knee and bleed. You might also want to bring money if you don't own any ice skates because you might need to rent some.

It is very important that you go in the winter because it is much colder and the ice is more frozen. Bring a sweater or jacket. You should also bring gloves because when you fall your fingers might stick to the ice a little bit. I would say go on Christmas or Christmas Eve because it gets colder on those days. January is the best time for ice skating because it is the coldest month. And like I said, go in the winter, not the summer.

I have some helpful tips so you know some places to go and practice your ice skating. You can go to Riis Park. Or, if you live too far you can go to Millennium Park, which is located in downtown Chicago. If you're too lazy like me to get up and drive too far, go to Lincoln Park or Navy Pier, which doesn't cost much. If you're not sure where to go, you might want to visit one of these places.

If you don't want to go alone, I'll help you. You can take your sister or brother or mom and Dad. Ice skating is also good for celebrating your birthday with your family.

When I went, I went with my dad and my sister, and we had a terrific time. One problem was that my dad tripped and then all of us almost fell on top of each other, just like we were in a hockey game. If you go on Valentine's Day, you should take your boyfriend or girlfriend. (Maybe you can get married!) Have a great time!

If you are bored and don't have anything to do go ice skating. It's fun. Go because you can actually entertain yourself and learn a new sport. Also, it's a very good experience. One day you might like it and take classes and become a champion. Have fun and enjoy ice skating! — *Alexis Vasquez, grade 4*

EVENTS

translations

» FROM PAGE 75

I FEEL LIKE I AM *in the* CLOUDS

ONE TIME, my family went to the restaurant, El Salvador. All of my family was happy there because it is very big and beautiful. If your family ever went to El Salvador, you would all be happy as well. You would shout for joy because it is so marvelous. I told my mom that I want to have a party there someday. I like it because the statues and the plants are very pretty. Many people go to El Salvador, but still it is charming. I feel like I am in the clouds there and I think that other people would feel like they were in the clouds too. All of the food is good. They have papusas, little tacos, and sandwiches. The rice, the beans, and the fruit are all special. The papusas they make are very delicious. All of my family is happy at the El Salvador restaurant. I hope that sometime more families can go and eat there. —*Tattiana Camargo, grade 3*

231

TRANSLATIONS

» FROM PAGE 94

WE MAKE THEM TOGETHER

232

MY MOM MAKES the most delicious tamales. Sometimes my mom cannot make them by herself and I help her so that she doesn't get tired. I pass the cornhusks to her to make the tamales. All of my family, including my aunts, uncles, cousins, and siblings like when my mom and I make tamales. We only make them for special occasions like birthdays. Every time we make tamales, my relatives say they are delicious. My mom likes to make tamales as much as I do. Tamales have corn meal, chicken, and meat sauce, these things make the tamales special. My mom makes the tamales with her hands and sometimes with utensils like a fork, spoon, and knife to cut the meat. I like tamales because my mom makes both sweet and green tamales. Sweet tamales have more flavor and green ones are a little green and white. I like to make tamales with my mom because we can do it together. If you are looking for my mom and me, you might be able to find us in the kitchen making tamales for a family birthday.   —*Yanet Morales, grade 4*

» FROM PAGE 98

A BALL *of* DELICIOUS FLAVORS

IT WAS A BEAUTIFUL DAY for my mom's thirty-second birthday. My dad ordered a chocolate cake. We called our friend's house. They arrived and we jumped on the bed and my mom said we had to be very careful not to fall. We jumped until we got tired. The cake arrived and we sang her Happy Birthday. The cake had little squares all over it. We sat down for fifteen minutes to let the food settle. We continued to play and also invited our neighbors over. My mom had made posole early that morning. Inside it was corn and a little brown strong coffee that gave it lots of flavor. It was a ball of delicious flavors. We ate posole and the smell was very good. Then people gave my mother many gifts. The guests announced that she was going to open her presents. She got a picture frame and money from my dad. The kids went home, then my family and I picked up the garbage. I watched TV, got my bed ready, and lay down to read a story about red shoes until I fell asleep.

—*Elizabeth Tellez, grade 3*

» FROM PAGE 99

THE RECIPE COMES *to* CHICAGO *from* MORELOS, MEXICO

WHENEVER MY AUNT has a party, she always tells my mom to bring posole. My aunt hosts all of the parties, because her house has a basement. Everyone else in the family brings food. I like when my mom makes posole because it smells delicious and tastes of corn, soup, avocado, small tortillas, eggs, lemons and lettuce or cabbage. When my mom makes posole, I help her peel the corn and I also watch to make sure the posole doesn't burn. I like to eat posole for special holidays, like birthdays, Christmas and New Year's. Posole smells of corn and soup and when my mom makes it in summer, the whole house gets very hot. My mom buys the supplies at Pete's. I think Pete's is on Archer Street.

The posole recipe comes from my family. My grandmother made the same posole in Mexico. The recipe comes to Chicago form Morelos, Mexico, the part of Mexico where my family is from. My family has been in the United States for fifteen years and we have always made my grandmother's posole.
—*Diana Benitez, grade 3*

» FROM PAGE 146

ICE CREAM *and* POPSICLES *with* YOUR FRIENDS

MCKINLEY PARK IS a fabulous place where one can have a big party and play with friends. It has a pool that is very big and another one for little kids and you can have a lot of fun. The pools are outside. During the winter they are closed. During the summer, you can eat ice cream and popsicles with your friends. Someone sells the food in a cart. You can play on the swings and there are some big ones and some small ones. There are slides. There is a big lake and near it you can play baseball. My cousin and I sometimes play baseball. My friend, Gaby, had a party there for her birthday. We played tag and hide and go seek outside in the park. Later, there was a magician and we goofed around a lot. Finally, we had a delicious chocolate cake with little figurines on top. If you are looking for a place to have a party, you should come to McKinley Park.

—*Susana Zavala, grade 3*

ABOUT *the* AUTHORS

SANTIAGO AGUILERA enjoys watching movies, especially when his whole family is with him. Santiago's favorite movie is *Everyone's Hero* and, every once in a while, he can be curiously heroic himself. *Namaste, Ms. Avitia's and Ms. Lola's second grade*

GABY (GABRIELA) AGUIRRE draws pictures because doing so cheers her up and makes her feel good about herself. She knows how to be a good friend and makes sure to keep her friends' secrets safe. *Casas, Ms. Heilman's sixth grade art class*

EZEKIEL ALBERTY is known to his classmates to be a good singer and actor. He is destined for the stage. *West Belden, Ms. Jacobson's fifth grade*

OLIVIA ALDEN gets to go to lots of Bulls games with her parents. Olivia claims that the best part of the game is jumping up and down when the Bulls score. *Alcott, Ms. Vincent's fifth grade*

MARYANN ALEJANDRE wants to help people and kids by being a doctor when she grows up. She is very impressed by her elementary school experience and thinks that her school has taught her well. *Casas, Ms. Heilman's second grade art class*

CHRISTOPHER ALFARO wants to be a policeman some day. He thinks that the public needs someone like him who can save them from villains. *Namaste, Ms. Avitia's and Ms. Lola's second grade*

ANTHONY ALVALADERO was told by his cousin that he should be on *Animal Planet* because of his extensive knowledge of animals. He has encyclopedic knowledge of fish. *West Belden, Ms. Jacobson's fifth grade*

LORENA ALVARADO loves animals and wants to be an animal doctor. She has several birds, one of which is soon going to have five babies. *West Belden, Ms. Micari's second grade*

DARLA ALVAREZ has many different personalities. Her hobbies include playing the guitar, singing, and acting. Darla is very careful to treat people with respect and dignity. *Casas, Ms. Heilman's fourth grade art class*

MICHAEL ANDERSON prides himself on his excellent sense of direction. He also can spell big words. Michael knows a lot about science and about outer space. *Casas, Ms. Heilman's fourth grade art class*

ARIANA APRIM wants to be a naturalist when she grows up. Ariana's role model is Steve the Crocodile Hunter because he goes everywhere and gets to touch the animals, even the dangerous ones. *Namaste, Ms. Frost's and Mr. Kelly's third grade*

IRVIN ARRELANO thinks his time is best spent hanging out with his family. In particular, he likes to play hopscotch with his mom and practice spelling with his dad. *West Belden, Ms. Tuzzolino's second grade*

JASMIN BAHENA gets excited just thinking about how much fun she has during summer vacation. She likes it when her family goes to the beach and they all pretend that they are sharks in the water. *Namaste, Ms. Avitia's and Ms. Lola's second grade*

ALEJANDRO BALLESTEROS moved to Chicago from Medellin, Colombia in 2001. When he was six, he learned to speak English by listening to his classmates. When Alejandro grows up, he wants to be a stock trader and work from home on his computer. *Courtenay, Ms. Metzger's fourth grade*

ALMA ROSA BANDA LEON likes playing with her sister and making art projects. She is very generous with her time and is always willing to help her friends and her classmates. *Casas, Ms. Heilman's second grade art class*

JACKY BANDA LEON loves to go to boxing matches and hopes to be a famous boxer or soldier one day. Jacky almost got straight A's once and never says anything bad about anyone. *Casas, Ms. Heilman's fifth grade art class*

HENRY BARRETT is committed to learning all he can about ancient Egypt. He is also a big fan of Abba. Henry is a strict vegetarian and has a pet gerbil named Jake. *Alcott, Ms. Tomczyk's fourth grade*

RICARDO BARRON enjoys spending quality time with his cousin and his sister. He is especially excited when that quality time involves watching wrestling matches. *West Belden, Ms. Tuzzolino's second grade*

ANDY BAUTISTA has one baby brother and one baby sister. They are a lot of work. Sometimes they confuse him by hiding from him and making a lot of trouble. *Courtenay, Ms. Metzger's fourth grade*

DIANA BENITEZ was born in Chicago but has an older sister who was born in Florida. Diana's birthday is August sixth. She is looking forward to it. *Lozano, Ms. Calderon's third grade*

HANNAH BERMAN loves to write stories about historical characters. She once wrote a story about a family that was in hiding during World War II. Her favorite book is *The Sea of Trolls* by Nancy Farmer. *Alcott, Ms. Vincent's fifth grade*

JAKIRA BLACK says she has a big family and she means it: she has five brothers and six sisters. Jakira loves being part of a family this size because there is always someone to play with. *Brownell, Ms. Maxim's sixth grade*

D'ASIA BLACKMON likes to sing church music and hip-hop. Her experience of fighting with her sister all of the time inspired her to want to become a lawyer when she grows up. This will help her to resolve conflicts peacefully. *Brownell, Ms. Kelly's fourth grade*

LUIS BLANCAS is proud of the fact that his mother and father are from Mexico. He is a big fan of his mother's cooking and loves spending time doing everyday things with his family. *Andersen, Ms. Rivera's third grade*

CARLOS BOTELLO is very glad that his mom showed him how to paint because now he wants to paint all of the time. He is particularly good at painting eagles and wolves in various settings. *Andersen, Ms. Rivera's third grade*

REBECA BRITO feels close to the animal world. She especially loves hamsters and dogs. At home she has a hamster named Chango. *Andersen, Ms. Schiff's second grade*

AYANNA BRYANT likes hip-hop and wants to be a professional singer and dancer when she grows up. Her favorite singer is Chris Brown. *Andersen, Ms. Hernandez's fifth grade*

BRITTANY BURRELL likes to play basketball, dance hip-hop, and learn about bodies. Brittany wants to be a basketball player and a teacher when she grows up. *West Belden, Ms. Monson's fifth grade*

EDDIE CALDERON is an early riser and likes to greet the day with activity. A great day for Eddie starts with playing football in the morning before going off to school. *Andersen, Ms. Hernandez's fifth grade*

TATTIANA CAMARGO está querida de toda su familia. También a ella le gusta leer. Su libro más favorito es *La Bellas Hijas de Mufaro*. Mufaro es un gran rey. »Tattiana is loved by her family. She also likes to read. Her favorite book is *The Beautiful Daughters of Mufaro*. Mufaro is a great king. *Namaste, Ms. Alvarado's and Ms. LeMont's third grade*

LESLIE CANET has two playful Chihuahuas. When she grows up, she wants to be a pet investigator so that she can go into people's houses and make sure their pets are being treated well. *Alcott, Ms. Klink's fifth grade*

AESHA CANO likes spending time with her family and going out to restaurants. She has one baby brother who is two years old. *Andersen, Ms. Schiff's second grade*

VICKY CANO says she may look American, but wants people to know that she is Mexican. Vicky likes to swim a lot and her favorite animal is a dog. *West Belden, Ms. Lynn's third grade*

LATASHIA CARDINE spends a lot of time dancing and thinking about dancing. Her favorite dance is "walk it out." She hopes one day to dance at the Apollo. *Brownell, Ms. Parker's sixth grade*

HAROLD CARPENTER claims to be hyperactive. He also loves to read and write about absolutely anything at all. One of Harold's favorite books is *The Lightening Thief. Pritzker, third grade, 826CHI workshop*

SEAN CARRILLO is a good artist. He likes to draw the high-speed hedgehog named Sonic. He draws Sonic in action poses, especially running and jumping. *Namaste, Ms. Avitia's and Ms. Lola's second grade*

JABARI CARROLL wouldn't come out and admit it, but he is very generous with his time. He is happy to help everyone that needs him in whatever way he can. *Andersen, Ms. Schiff's second grade*

VICTORIA CARUTH has two primary talents: solving cases and detecting when people are lying. She hopes to put these gifts to use by becoming a lawyer some day. *Brownell, Ms. Jones's fourth grade*

ANDREA CASTILLO is herself and nobody else. She wants to make sure people know that even when you think she might not be listening, she actually is. *Casas, Ms. Heilman's sixth grade art class*

ITZEL CASTILLO is on the swim team for the Chicago Park District. She also enjoys playing the violin and bike riding. Her favorite subject is history. *Home-schooled, fifth grade, 826CHI workshop*

JASMINE CASTILLO is often told that she is funny. She acts goofy, says hilarious things, and has an energetic personality. She loves to hang out with her friends and get them laughing. She also likes to read, especially non-fiction books. *Alcott, Ms. Billingham's sixth grade*

ALEX (ALEJANDRO) CHIQUITO likes to exercise and has a special personality. He is giving to his friends and will share anything he has with them. *Casas, Ms. Heilman's fifth grade art class*

ODESSA CODY is a high-flying gymnast and an animal lover. She has a big family with lots of people to love and take care of her. She loves chocolate ice cream sundaes from Margie's. *Pritzker, fifth grade, 826CHI workshop*

MIGUEL CORIA earns money by helping his dad, a tow-truck driver. Miguel's job involves writing down the names, phone numbers, and addresses of people who call and need to have their cars towed. *Courtenay, Ms. Kiley's fifth grade*

AURORA CORREA really likes math because it comes so easily to her. Whenever the teacher explains something, she gets it right away and always answers all of the questions. Aurora almost never gets a question wrong. *Andersen, Ms. Ryan's fourth grade*

NICOLE CULVER has lots of hobbies. On Wednesdays, she sings in a choir. She used to play chess on Wednesdays as well, but now chess is over. *Blaine, second grade, 826CHI workshop*

ADRIANA DAVIS has written quite a few books for little kids. She already has a plan for her next book, which will be called *One Day at the Park. Namaste, Ms. Alvarado's and Ms. LaMont's third grade*

NAZIR DAVIS likes writing books. He also likes basketball. His favorite team is the Bulls and he has even seen Michael Jordan. *Andersen, Ms. Schiff's second grade*

MELANIE DE LA CRUZ knows how to keep five kids under the age of seven in one place. "Popcorn is the key," she says. *West Belden, Ms. Monson's fifth grade*

EDUARDO DELGADO loves to play wrestling video games. He is also a homework fanatic. Some days Eduardo would even rather stay at home and do more homework than come to school. *West Belden, Ms. Lynn's third grade*

MELISSA DELGADO is very quiet because she is always thinking up good ideas. Her teacher has told her that she has very neat handwriting. *Andersen, Ms. Ryan's fourth grade*

MARIO DIAZ likes that his name is from a video game. He also knows how to laugh just like Sponge Bob. *West Belden, Ms. Lynn's third grade*

CHRISTOPHER DIAZ DE LEON likes playing games like checkers, and his friends say he is smart. He wants to use his intelligence to be a top policeman one day. *Lozano, Ms. Rudnick's second grade*

TASIA DRAKE takes dance classes on Saturdays and Sundays. Once, her class performed in a dance competition and they won three hundred dollars. Tasia went on a shopping spree with her winnings. *Alcott, Ms. Klink's fifth grade*

JOSHUA ESTERS is a bit of a practical joker. He likes to scare people with his Navy Seal gear. Joshua claims the best time for playing tricks is the summer. *Brownell, Ms. Shea's third grade*

AUTUMN EVINS likes to draw anything that is out of the ordinary. She really likes little dogs, like Chihuahuas, because they are light enough to hold. Autumn also has a keen eye for fashion. *Namaste, Ms. Frost's and Mr. Kelly's third grade*

YULISA FLORES enjoys spending time with her friends and her older brother. She is happiest when she is listening to stories or drawing pictures. *Andersen, Ms. Silva's second grade*

SYLVIA FRANK loves to write fairy tales and life stories. She once wrote a short story, "Little Yellow Rough Riding Hood," which involved a troll, a basket of pasta, and a broom closet. *Alcott, Ms. Cameron's fourth grade*

KIRA GALLANCY loves watching dolphins do tricks because they can jump so high. At one of the shows, she got to feed fish to the dolphins. *Alcott, Ms. Tomczyk's fourth grade*

JAIME GARCIA was born in Michoacan, Mexico. He loves soccer. Jaime also loves math and can't figure out why nobody else does. *West Belden, Ms. Monson's fifth grade*

JENNIFER GARCIA wants to be a singer and an art teacher when she grows up. She is always careful to respect her friends' feelings. *Casas, Ms. Heilman's fifth grade art class*

ISABELLA GARDUÑO estimates that there are two hundred people in her family. In addition to many relatives, Isabella has a cat named Jennifer that rolls around on the floor. Isabella wants to be a mom when she grows up. *Lozano, Ms. Scampini's third grade*

DARYL GATEWOOD loves football and has decided he would like to be in the National Football League. Brian Urlacher is his favorite player and Daryl looks to him for inspiration. *Brownell, Ms. Maxim's sixth grade*

JOSE GATICA would like to be a famous soccer player when he grows up. He would play for Chivas and would make a superb goalie. *West Belden, Ms. Bartgen's third grade*

KAREN GAYTAN wants to learn how to play volleyball. When she turned nine years old, her mom gave her Samantha, the American Girl doll. Karen was quite thrilled. *Andersen, Ms. Maloney's third grade*

SAMUEL GHANSAH likes to watch movies about warriors, like *A Knight's Tale*. He loves to run and usually runs about a mile. *Alcott, Ms. Tomczyk's fourth grade*

KRYSTAL GILES may only be in fifth grade, but she is a world-class chef. She likes to cook chicken, macaroni and cheese, and potatoes. Krystal can prepare potatoes in both the mashed and baked forms. *Brownell, Ms. Kemble's fifth grade*

KYETREL GLASS likes to travel to Michigan and Detroit to visit family and to see the sights. She'd like to be a doctor and help children because she once met a little girl who had cancer and it made her think. *Brownell, Ms. Kelly's fourth grade*

BRANDON GNIADEK wants to be a cop because he watches cop shows and it gets him interested. He also likes the prince characters in Disney movies and really enjoys eating Skittles. *Lozano, Ms. Scampini's third grade*

JENNY GONZALEZ likes to draw and listen to Spanish music. She wants to play basketball but thinks that she is a little too short. *Alcott, Ms. Billingham's sixth grade*

NIKOLAS GONZALEZ likes to travel. He also enjoys drawing things that he sees around him, such as his bedroom dresser. Someday Nikolas would like to return to Puerto Rico. *West Belden, Ms. Szot's fourth grade*

COLETTE GORDON absolutely loves writing, drawing, violin, and soccer. Her favorite authors are J.K. Rowling and Roald Dahl. Colette's friends know that they are very important to her because she tells them often. *La Salle, second grade, 826CHI workshop*

DANISHA GREYER likes to go out with her family so she can get to know them better. She goes with her mom, two aunts, two grandmas, three uncles, four sisters, four brothers, and six cousins to Old Country Buffet. It is delicious there. *Brownell, Ms. Kelly's fourth grade*

ANGEL GUEVARA likes to learn new things like roller skating. Angel can jump on roller skates, spin, and go backwards. He has two dogs. When Angel comes home from school, the dogs get so excited that they do flips. *Namaste, Ms. Frost's and Mr. Kelly's third grade*

DYLAN HADDAD likes to ride his bike after school. He meets other kids at the park and they ride around on their scooters or skateboards together. *Alcott, Ms. Billingham's sixth grade*

NAJA HARRINGTON likes writing and wants to be an author of kids' books. Her first book was called *The Haunted House. Andersen, Ms. Maloney's third grade*

ASHLEY HARRIS greatly enjoys spending time with her family. She likes to hang out in the park and swing so high on the swings that she nearly touches the trees. *Brownell, Ms. Jones's fourth grade*

MELISSA HARVEY loves to eat food that excites her taste buds. She also considers it important to stay healthy. *Brownell, Ms. Kemble's fifth grade*

KATHY HERNANDEZ is a very good student and wants to be an artist when she grows up. Her favorite thing to do after school is to play with her dad. Kathy works hard to never get mad at her friends. *Casas, Ms. Heilman's second grade art class*

NATALIE HERNANDEZ practices Tae Kwan Do two times a week. Right now she has a white belt, but pretty soon she is going to get her yellow one. *Lozano, Ms. Scampini's third grade*

KEVIN HERNANDEZ CORTEZ has a biting turtle called Chico who likes to eat lettuce. Chico doesn't bite Kevin because Kevin is nice. Chico walks around Kevin's house and usually falls asleep on the couch. *Namaste, Ms. Frost's and Mr. Kelly's third grade*

MARIO HERRERA is nine years old, and when he grows up he wants to be a policeman in Chicago. His uncle is a policeman and has inspired him to catch bad guys. *Lozano, Ms. Scampini's third grade*

JASMINE HINES enjoys writing stories about things she does with her granddaddy. They have fun playing games like Connect Four and Boggle, and have even gone to Texas. *Brownell, Ms. Kelly's fourth grade*

MELODI HOFF likes herself, especially her teeth. She looked like a boy when she was a baby, but then she grew up. Melodi would like to be an artist. *Namaste, Ms. Schwarnweber's and Ms. English's third grade*

NADEJA HOLLOWAY is a proud member of a choir. She also likes to dance to hip-hop music. When she goes to church, she helps to lead the singing there. *West Belden, Ms. Bartgen's third grade*

DAIJA JACKSON very much enjoys spending time riding around with her brother in the car. They particularly like watching the tall buildings go by. *Brownell, Ms. Kelly's fourth grade*

CURTIA JAMES likes writing. She even had her book, *The Big Test*, published by her school. *The Big Test* is about her dream ISAT test. *Andersen, Ms. Ziegler's fifth grade class*

JASMIN JIMENEZ likes drawing for fun when she has finished her homework. She likes making her artwork as colorful as she can. *Lozano, Ms. Scampini's third grade*

JUAN JIMENEZ went to Wisconsin for his birthday in July. He went with his Aunt and Uncle and Cousins and had a great time. *Andersen, Ms. Schiff's second grade*

SEBASTIAN JIMENEZ likes to play soccer in the sand with his friends. In the summer, you can often find him swimming in the lake. *Courtenay, Ms. Gonsalves's sixth grade*

STEPHANY JIMENEZ is proud of her mom for being so nice, working so hard, and taking such good care of her. *Andersen, Ms. Hernandez's fifth grade*

ZACHARY JOINER has super parents who give him lots of hugs. Zachary likes playing baseball and his favorite team is the Cubs. *Lozano, Ms. Rudnick's second grade*

YASMIN JONES has plenty more stories about strange chickens like the one that she shared in this book. One of her stories is a cliffhanger about the scary chicken following her around the restaurant. *Andersen, Ms. Maloney's third grade*

TRISTAN KAGAN is the only one who likes playing tennis in his class. He is carrying on the tradition from his dad and grandpa who also like playing the game. *Alcott, Ms. Vincent's fifth grade*

RAMSHA KHAWAR takes care of her rabbit, two parakeets, and goldfish. She wants to grow up to be a basketball coach on the weekends and an artist during the week. *Alcott, Ms. Vincent's fifth grade*

PAULETTA KELLEY does her homework every day and gets good grades in class. Pauletta considers herself to be an expert on compound words. Her favorite compound word is "somewhere" because she likes to go places. *Brownell, Ms. Shea's third grade*

DALE KENDRICK spends time with his family playing Uno and the Play Station game, Spy Hunter. He wants to be a policeman in Chicago so that he can help people all over the city. *Brownell, Ms. Parker's fifth grade*

SAMANTHA KOSLOSKE plays soccer and is especially good at midfield defense. She likes making collages, and usually uses a combination of photos and stickers. *Alcott, Ms. Vincent's fifth grade*

ALEAH KRAFT was named after an artist, Aleah Korey, who paints pictures of flowers with all sorts of colors. Aleah likes being named after an artist because when she grows up, she wants to be an artist herself. *Alcott, Ms. Tomczyk's fourth grade*

NIA LEE has a hamster named Max. Max loves to run on his wheel and tries to escape. Nia also loves rabbits and, when she lived in California, she had a very special rabbit named Fred. *Alcott, Ms. Vincent's fifth grade*

ESTEBAN LICEA is extremely organized and good at drawing. After school, he enjoys playing outside in the fresh air with his brother. *Casas, Ms. Heilman's fourth grade art class*

JAMELL LINCOLN has two sisters and four brothers and he enjoys being the youngest of them all. Jamell refuses to eat black eyed peas, which he claims are nasty, even though he has never eaten one. *Brownell, Ms. Parker's sixth grade*

JOCELYNE LUNA loves chocolate very much. She also likes to play hockey in gym class, which is also her favorite subject in school. *Lozano, Ms. Scampini's third grade*

CHARLES LYANG is an energetic fan of the White Sox. He also admits, after some prodding, that he actually likes the Yankees as well. Charles also is intrigued by tropical fish. *Mark Sheridan, sixth grade, 826CHI workshop*

JEFFREY LYANG travels a lot! He has been to Yellowstone, Arizona, New York, Montana, South Dakota, Ohio, and China, but says that he would rather stay home and play. He has one brother and his favorite animal is the dolphin. *Mark Sheridan, third grade, 826CHI workshop*

BOYÉ MCCARTHY says that his mom's cooking has inspired him to want to be a chef. He started cooking when he was six years old. His first dish was pancakes. *Brownell, Ms. Kemble's fifth grade*

SHEILA MCINTOSH was born on Pluto in the year 2008 and sent her essay back in time by satyr. When Sheila grows up she wants to be a dragon. *Pritzker, fifth grade, 826CHI workshop*

UROOJ MAHMOOD likes school but would never pass up the chance to skip for a day to celebrate holidays from his home country of Pakistan. Eid is an example of one such holiday and it happens at the end of the year. *Courtenay, Ms. Gonsalves's sixth grade*

ULISES MALDONADO swims underwater in a pool and likes to jump in the water in the deep end. He swims with his big cousin and his little cousins, a boy and a girl. *West Belden, Ms. Micari's second grade*

NICOLE MANRIQUEZ likes to write a lot and has two poems published in a children's magazine. *Andersen, Ms. Hernandez's fifth grade*

JULIAN MARTINEZ is in the sixth grade class and likes to play sports, play video games, and have fun. She also likes to collect stuff like cards, souvenirs, and little cars. *Newberry, sixth grade, 826CHI workshop*

CARI E. MATOS is usually shy about singing, but she once sang in a talent show when she was seven. Cari also loves to write, and in her third grade class, she wrote a story about three mean girls and one lonely, small girl. *Courtenay, Ms. Gonsalves's sixth grade*

JUSTIN MATHEWS can make his ears move without touching them. He has been in a few musicals and considers himself to be very talented at the game of charades. *Brownell, Ms. Kemble's fifth grade*

ANDREW MAYEN wants to be an FBI agent when he grows up so that he can round up criminals from the streets. *Andersen, Ms. Ryan's fourth grade*

CESAR MELENDEZ really likes to read books about sports. He especially likes books about football. His favorite football team is the Chicago Bears. *Andersen, Ms. Maloney's third grade*

KEVIN MENDEL likes all kinds of jets and wants to be a pilot some day. Kevin likes to visit his uncle in New York City and hopes to travel to Ireland soon. *Blaine, second grade, 826CHI workshop*

KATIE MENDEZ has three dogs. Cookie is a Shitzu-Poodle; Bugsy is a Pug; and Nikita is a Siberian Husky-Border Collie. *West Belden, Ms. Jacobson's fifth grade*

EDUARDO MENTADO is big. He has a new red and black bike and he likes to get around on it. Eduardo enjoys riding his bike in the park and also in front of his house. *Andersen, Ms. Silva's second grade*

ROSENDO METADO likes to ride his skateboard at the skate park and in his backyard in the summer time. Rosendo says that riding a skateboard feels just like you are floating. *Andersen, Ms. Hernandez's fifth grade*

ARITEJA MILLER is very active. She likes basketball and other games that she can play outside. She is fond of freeze tag as well. *Lozano, Ms. Rudnick's second grade*

BRITTANY MILLS is very energetic and sees things differently than all the other kids. She always sees a different way to solve a problem. She thinks this is maybe because she pays attention to her mom and teacher. *Alcott, Ms. Klink's fifth grade*

RASHAD MITCHELL likes to sing in the shower and in the car. He is going to get a cat soon and wants to name it Little Rashad. *Brownell, Ms. Maxim's sixth grade*

HECTOR MONTALVO wants to be a silk printer like his brother, Adrian, when he grows up. Hector is trustworthy and he is almost always happy. *Casas, Ms. Heilman's fifth grade art class*

DAVID MONTE DE OCA has two brothers and a sister. He likes riding his bike with his brothers in the park. *West Belden, Ms. Tuzzolino's second grade*

ZACH MOORE is really good at playing video games. He can usually get through about half the levels in half an hour. He is going to ask his friends to coach him so that he can get to be even better. *Alcott, Ms. Vincent's fifth grade*

ANTONIO MORALES wants to be a cop when he grows up because he thinks he'd be pretty good at saving people. Antonio's best friend is Enrique. Enrique is fun and funny. *Namaste, Ms. Alvarado's and Ms. LaMont's third grade*

NATALIA MORALES likes to spend time with her family and has a twin brother in her class. Natalia also like to write poems and draw pictures. *Namaste, Ms. Avitia's and Ms. Lola's second grade*

YANET MORALES tiene dos hermanos y dos hermanas. Ella le gusta hacer su tarea especialmente lectura. Su libro favorito es *Sobre, los Tamales.* »Yanet has two brothers and two sisters. She likes to do her homework, especially reading. Her favorite book is *About Tamales. Lozano, Ms. Calderon's third grade*

DAJA MULLEN likes to bother her teacher. Once Daja hid behind a desk and scared her. The teacher thought it was funny. *Brownell, Ms. Kelly's fourth grade*

MARIA MURILLO has a talent for blowing bubbles. The biggest bubble she ever blew was the size of her face. It popped after it floated away. *Lozano, Ms. Rudnick's second grade*

ELENA MURO considers herself to be nice and feels that she is rather graceful. She has nine nationalities in her family. *Casas, Ms. Heilman's second grade art class*

LI NGUYEN wants to be a veterinarian when she grows up because she likes animals. She likes all animals and would help any that needed her assistance, but she has a soft spot for birds. *Andersen, Ms. Ryan's fourth grade*

ARELI NUÑEZ is eight years old and loves to read chapter books, especially ones about dinosaurs and science. Her favorite dinosaur is the T. Rex because he is big and scary. *Lozano, Ms. Calderon's third grade*

CYNTHIA OCHOA has a new dog. It's almost like a Chihuahua and its name is Lady. Cynthia's mom is going to have a baby soon and Cynthia is pretty sure it will be a boy. *Andersen, Ms. Silva's second grade*

ROSA OCHOA admits that she can talk a lot. Rosa wants to be a doctor when she grows up so that she can make kids who are sick feel better. She also loves to dance. *Casas, Ms. Heilman's sixth grade art class*

ISAI OLIVARES likes to play football. He throws very straight and nobody intercepts his passes. Isai learned how to throw a football straight by studying the techniques of Peyton Manning. *West Belden, Ms. Jacobson's fifth grade*

NESTOR ORTIZ never gives up! He thinks of each test in school as a fight. If he gets a C, he keeps on trying and trying until he gets an A. *West Belden, Ms. Monson's fifth grade*

YEMISI OSOSAMI came from Nigeria, Africa about one year ago. Yemisi wants to become a doctor so that she can go back to Nigeria and help people. *Andersen, Ms. Ryan's fourth grade*

SAMANTHA OVIEDO has a lot of pets. She has two turtles, three cats, and a dog. The turtles, sadly, have no names. The dog is named Nico, and the cats are named Charko, Fluffy, and Duma. *West Belden, Ms. Lynn's third grade*

JAIME PALAFOX finds much pleasure in running around the park and winning basketball championships. He also can move his knuckles around while he is making a fist. *Casas, Ms. Heilman's fourth class art class*

KRYSTAL PEÑA feels special to be the largest girl in the third grade class. Her cousins and her grandma live in Mexico and they have four dogs. They all live in one big house. *Namaste, Ms. Alvarado's and Ms. LaMont's third grade*

EDUARDO PEREZ wants to be a famous racecar driver when he grows up. He has a ton of cousins who live in Mexico. *Lozano, Ms. Calderon's fourth grade*

SERGIO PEREZ is going to Mexico this summer to play with his cousins and friends. They really like to play hide-and-seek and soccer. *West Belden, Ms. Micari's second grade*

JOSUE PORTILLO loves video games. In fact, he has a PSP and a PS2 and a DS. He also knows a lot about cars. *West Belden, Ms. Szot's fourth grade*

HENRY POST likes bugs even though everybody else hates them. He saves every bug that he can. He once saved a water bug that was drowning. *Courtenay, Ms. Metzger's fourth grade*

OLYVIA PUENTE knows sign language. Her uncle got her interested because he had to learn it for his job as a police officer. She wants to be a sign language interpreter at an airport. *Courtenay, Ms. Kiley's fifth grade*

SARAH QUANDER is a ballet dancer, and has been dancing for three and a half years. She was in *The Nutcracker* in the Auditorium Theater. She has one brother, one sister, and a dog named Quaygon. *Alcott, Ms. Vincent's fifth grade*

IAN QUIROZ has four brothers. He is the second oldest. Ian's favorite thing to do after school is play soccer with his dad. Ian's dad is from Mexico and teaches him everything he knows about soccer. *Courtenay, Ms. Gonsalves's sixth grade*

BRENDA RAMIREZ is sometimes a good family member. Sometimes she helps her mom clean up her room or her brother clean up the dishes. Sometimes, though, her brother bothers her and she gets mad and yells at him. She even pushes him once in a while. *West Belden, Ms. Lynn's third grade*

FERNANDO RAMIREZ GAYTAN is Mexican and loves to play goalie and forward in soccer. He used to be a straight-A student and wants to be again so he can go to college and become a game designer. *West Belden, Ms. Monson's fifth grade*

JIMENA RAZO wants to be a teacher because teachers get to show their students a lot. Teachers also get to take their students on field trips, which Jimena enjoys. *Lozano, Ms. Calderon's third grade*

STEFANY REBOLLAR has four big brothers and two nieces already, but no sisters. She is the littlest girl and the only girl. She likes to swim whenever and wherever she can. *West Belden, Ms. Joyce's fourth grade*

DAVID RENTERIA loves to play basketball because he is kind of good at it. Sometimes his mom makes pepperoni pizza that is spicy, tasty, and hot. *West Belden, Ms. Lynn's third grade*

CRYSTAL REYES has really good grades and likes to play hockey or sports of any kind. *Andersen, Ms. Ziegler's fifth grade*

JONATHAN RIVAS wants to play professional soccer. His favorite team is Brazil. Ronaldinho Gaucho is his favorite player. *Lozano, Ms. Calderon's fourth grade*

SELENA RIVERA loves dogs and loves taking care of them. She has a dog named Buddy who is a golden retriever. *Andersen, Ms. Hernandez's fifth grade*

JENNIXHIA RODRIGUEZ really likes playing and laughing with her family. One of her favorite times to do this is at family reunions. *Andersen, Ms. Hernandez's fifth grade*

MELANIE ROLON doesn't like noise, especially tires squealing, air planes roaring, and the bus. She likes silence around the city. *Lozano, Ms. Scampini's third grade*

MICHAEL ROMAN loves to play Legos and spend time with his family. He loves to do math lessons and likes to compete with his friends in soccer matches. *Andersen, Ms. Silva's second grade*

IVETTE RUCOBO is unique because she is not the same size as anyone else. She wants to be a doctor when she gets older and is very good at doing origami. *Casas, Ms. Heilman's fourth grade art class*

EILEEN SALAS is pretty good at drawing. The last thing she did was a sketch of Johnny Depp from *Pirates of the Caribbean*. She also feels that she can draw a pretty impressive Orlando Bloom. *Alcott, Ms. Cameron's fourth grade*

DIANA SALGADO is really active. She likes to play a lot and has a lot of energy. Diana is a big fan of games that involve running, like tag. *West Belden, Ms. Joyce's fourth grade*

NORMA SANCE has two sisters and a brother. She likes to play with her large dog, Tinny, outside. *Andersen, Ms. Hernandez's fifth grade*

DIANA SANCHEZ likes to help people, especially little kids who need homework help, or friends in her class. She answers other people's questions too—just ask! *Courtenay, Ms. Gonsalves's sixth grade*

JORGE SANTOS likes playing basketball, baseball, and football. He is also a good artist. Jorge's father is from Mexico, and his mother is from Guatemala. *West Belden, Ms. Jacobson's fifth grade*

JOSHUA SERRANO plays soccer. He is the goalie and his whole family comes to watch him play. One time, a seventeen-year-old boy couldn't make a goal on him. Joshua hit the ball away, and his team won! *Namaste, Ms. Schwarnweber's and Ms. English's second grade*

MALIK SHAW has decided that he wants to be a dentist. He wants to help people with their teeth. Malik likes playing video games like Dragon Ball Z. *Namaste, Ms. Schwarnweber's and Ms. English's second grade*

EKYRA SINGLETON likes to draw special things like flowers and roses. She likes to swim in the pool in the spring and summertime. *West Belden, Ms. Tuzzolino's second grade*

JUSTICE SMITH greatly enjoys going to gymnastics. She likes to do tricks on the bar, but she often falls on her butt. She has better luck on the mats, where she can do cartwheels and flips. *Andersen, Ms. Ryan's fourth grade*

FAITH STEIN is very passionate about writing and has written more books in her lifetime than she can count. Faith has participated in her school's Young Authors contest every year since first grade class. *Blaine, second grade, 826CHI workshop*

JUAN SUAREZ loves to play soccer and has great ball handling skills as a forward. His team won twenty-seven games last year! *Andersen, Ms. Ziegler's fifth grade*

MAHNOOR SYED loves animals, especially tigers and lambs. She enjoys drawing and wants to be a meteorologist some day. *Alcott, Ms. Cameron's fourth grade*

JACQUELINE TAPIA is a good artist and likes to draw trolls. The girl trolls have gems on their belly buttons and magical spell beads. *West Belden, Ms. Micari's second grade*

ELIZABETH TELLEZ le gusta penar al pelo. Ella tiene una muñeca y peina su pelo. »Elizabeth likes to brush hair. She has a doll and brushes her hair. *Andersen, Ms. Rivera's third grade*

MYLIAH TERRY is an only child. She is a dancer in a hip-hop group and has been on TV. Her favorite song to dance to is called "Party Time," by Missy Elliot. Myliah dances at least two hours each week. *Alcott, Ms. Billingham's sixth grade*

LEVI TODD wants to be a writer of adventurous books. His favorite series is called *Kidnapped* and it is very suspenseful. *Courtenay, Ms. Kiley's fifth grade*

HEIDI TORRES was inspired to be a great illustrator by her brother because he is good at drawing. She doesn't know if he'll agree, but she thinks she is already better than her brother! *Andersen, Ms. Ziegler's fifth grade*

JANICE TORRES knows that the secret to being a good friend is being sure of yourself. She thinks her family is special and unique. *Casas, Ms. Heilman's third grade art class*

NICHOLAS TOVAR likes to ride his bike around Soldier Field and Grant Park. His friends often come to him for advice or to get cheered up. He doesn't let his friends talk about each other behind their backs. *Alcott, Ms. Billingham's sixth grade*

JOHNESHA TURNER likes to write stories about people she doesn't know. She is an only child and is very good at crossing the monkey bars. *Brownell, Ms. Elfer's third grade*

BETTY TYLER draws cartoons with colored pencils and is currently making a comic book. She recently invented a character that is a combination of a butterfly and a mouse. *Andersen, Ms. Ziegler's fifth grade*

MAICO UZHCA likes to play soccer at Riis Park with his friends after school. He is a pretty fast runner. *Andersen, Ms. Ziegler's fifth grade*

KIMBERLY VALDEZ has a brother who is seven and a dog whose name is Tyson. The dog is eight months old and loves to chase his tail in circles. *Courtenay, Ms. Kiley's fifth grade*

LUIS VALENCIANO is a smart kid who is good at math. When he is not being good at math he is break-dancing with his group. *West Belden, Ms. Joyce's fourth grade*

OLIVIA VANOVERBEKE likes to go roller skating in Round Lake, near where her grandmother lives. She also likes to go wake boarding and goes to a wake boarding and horseback riding camp every summer. *Alcott, Ms. Tomczyk's fourth grade*

ALEXIS VASQUEZ laughs a lot and smiles even more. You almost have to see it to believe it. Alexis likes to draw and takes requests from her audience. She drew a spectacular castle once. *West Belden, Ms. Joyce's fourth grade*

IVONNE VASQUEZ wants to be an artist so that she can paint and do sculpture. She has a big family tree but everyone outside of her immediate family lives in Mexico. *Andersen, Ms. Ryan's fourth grade*

EDUARDO VEGA is good at every sport, but his favorite sport is basketball. Last year he played basketball a lot at Pulaski Park. *Lozano, Ms. Cline's fourth grade*

VIRGINIA VELARDE has one brother who is her twin. She says that he is her evil twin, but she is only joking. She likes him a lot, even though he sleepwalks. *West Belden, Ms. Bartgen's third grade*

DANNY VIGIL, JR. loves to do his math homework after school. He considers himself to be a good friend because he helps people when they're hurt. *Casas, Ms. Heilman's second grade art class*

JOCELYN VILLA is a very happy person who loves to write poems and stories. She has a great family that encourages her in what she wants to do. *West Belden, Ms. Jacobson's fifth grade*

JONATAN VILLA is ten years old and he loves to play soccer. If Jonathan had to eat the same food for lunch everyday, it would be plain cheese pizza. He likes to read *Captain Underpants* books because they are super funny. *Lozano, Ms. Cline's fourth grade*

HOGUER VILLADA shares all of his things with his friends, which makes him feel happy and proud. He also has a crazy Chihuahua named Brownie who likes to play with other people and to bark. *West Belden, Ms. Szot's fourth grade*

JULIANNA VILLAREAL wants to become a veterinarian. She wants to take care of animals, especially puppies and dogs, because she likes them so much. *Namaste, Ms. Frost's and Mr. Kelly's third grade*

NOE VILLEDA wants to play football for the Bears in the position of wide receiver. He plays catch with his dad as training. *Andersen, Ms. Ryan's fourth grade*

LIZZIE WALSH has a gerbil named Minnie. Lizzie wants to be a professional skateboarder someday and write fantasy novels. *Alcott, Ms. Tomczyk's fourth grade*

DONTE WASHINGTON likes to play the video game Take Out all night, or at least until 10:00 p.m. The game has a lot of action in it. It is just like the army. *West Belden, Ms. Bartgen's third grade*

ROYAL WASHINGTON likes everything that involves reading: books, magazines and the newspapers. Royal likes model cars because they're shiny and some of them are fast. Often he'll sketch a car before he builds it. *Alcott, Ms. Cameron's fourth grade*

TIERRA WASHINGTON has three sisters, four brothers, and fifty-eight cousins. Because she can't decide between them, Tierra would like to work three jobs when she grows up: police officer, doctor, and lawyer. *Brownell, Ms. Parker's sixth grade*

SHADELL WHITE likes to jump rope and especially likes double dutch with her friends. According to Shadell, the best place for jumping rope is the park at 71ˢᵗ Street. There is a lot of room there and nothing gets in your way. *Brownell, Ms. Kelly's fourth grade*

JEREMY WILSON wants to be a scientist and an inventor. He has an excellent plan for a rocket car in his mind and will make sure that it is non-polluting. *West Belden, Ms. Micari's second grade*

MARCUS YEE wants to be a doctor when he grows up. His dad is a nurse and has taught him a lot about the human body and how it works. *Courtenay, Ms. Kiley's fifth grade*

ANDRES ZAVALA likes to draw and is especially talented at sketching scenes of ocean life. Andres likes to tell jokes and is, admittedly, rather funny. *Casas, Ms. Heilman's third grade class art class*

SUSANA ZAVALA le gusta ayudar a sus mascotas. Ella tiene un gato que se llama Tisok. Ella quiere un conjejo y un perrito. »Susana likes to help her pets. She has a cat named Tisok. She wants a rabbit and a small dog. *Namaste, Ms. Alvarado's and Ms. LeMont's third grade*

VICTOR ZAVALA likes to write in cursive and, when he wants to, can act pretty goofy. Reading and drawing both relax him and he will never backstab his friends. *Casas, Ms. Heilman's sixth grade art class*

ABOUT 826CHI

826CHI is a non-profit organization dedicated to supporting students ages six to eighteen with their creative and expository writing skills, and to helping teachers inspire their students to write. Our services are structured around our belief that great leaps in learning can happen with one-on-one attention, and that strong writing skills are fundamental to future success. With this in mind we provide drop-in tutoring, after-school workshops, in-schools tutoring, help for English language learners, and assistance with student publications. All of our programs are challenging and enjoyable, and ultimately strengthen each student's power to express ideas effectively, creatively, confidently, and in his or her individual voice.

. . .

OUR PROGRAMS

DROP-IN TUTORING
Every Monday through Thursday during the school year, from 3:00 until 5:30 p.m., we offer free drop-in tutoring. During this time, 826CHI is bustling with students who come by to work on

homework, to do research, or to engage in our daily creative writing activities. No task is too big or too small for our tutors. Pre-registration is not required. Students should just show up, ready to work.

FIELD TRIPS

We want to help teachers get their students excited about writing while also helping students to better express their ideas. We invite teachers to bring their classes to our site for high-energy field trips during the school days. A group of tutors is on-hand during every field trip, whether we are helping to generate new material or revise already written work. To sign up, please visit our website.

WORKSHOPS

826CHI has a broad base of tutors who are experts in many different areas of writing. Our tutors are skilled in journalism, song writing, comic book production, radio broadcasting and a variety of other subjects. These tutors offer specialized writing workshops several times per week, during evenings and on weekends. Our current offerings are available at www.826chi.org.

IN-SCHOOLS ASSISTANCE

The strength of our volunteer base allows us to partner with Chicago area schools. 826CHI will send volunteers into local schools to support teachers with projects in their own classroom. If you are a teacher who needs extra help revising research papers, writing college entrance exams, or editing your school newspaper, contact us through our website. 826CHI will dispatch a group of volunteers that will arrive, ready to work one-on-one.

PUBLISHING

826CHI believes that the quality of student work is greatly enhanced when students are allowed to share their writing with an authentic audience. Therefore, we're committed to giving students an outlet for the original work that they produce, whether it be in their own personal publication that we bind in-house, or in a specially produced volume such as this one.

THE BORING STORE

826CHI shares a space with The Boring Store, Chicago's only undercover secret agent supply store. The Boring Store offers spy supplies in a most secretive way. We have grappling hooks; we have envelope x-ray spray; and we have an ever-expanding array of fake moustaches. We also have heavy surveillance at the door. All proceeds from The Boring Store go directly toward supporting 826CHI's free writing programs for Chicago students.

• • •

Please visit www.826chi.org *to find out more about our programs, our schedule, and how to get involved.*